MICROCOSM PUBLISHING is Portland's most diversified publishing house and distributor, with a focus on the colorful, authentic, and empowering. Our books and zines have put your power in your hands since 1996, equipping readers to make positive changes in their lives and in the world around them. Microcosm emphasizes skill-building, showing hidden histories, and fostering creativity through challenging conventional publishing wisdom with books and bookettes about DIY skills, food, bicycling, gender, self-care, and social justice. What was once a distro and record label started by Joe Biel in a drafty bedroom was determined to be *Publishers Weekly*'s fastest-growing publisher of 2022 and #3 in 2023, and is now among the oldest independent publishing houses in Portland, OR, and Cleveland, OH. We are a politically moderate, centrist publisher in a world that has inched to the right for the past 80 years.

Ghouls Rule

A Celebration of Female Movie Monsters

Emma Alice Johnson

MICROCOSM PUBLISHING
Portland, Oregon | Cleveland, Ohio

GHOULS RULE

A Celebration of Female Movie Monsters

First edition - 2,000 copies - August 4, 2026
ISBN 9781648416293
This is Microcosm #1057
Edited by Ivy Zeller
Designed by Joe Biel and Sarah Koch

All the news from the misfits in print at Microcosm.Pub/Newsletter
Get more copies of this book at Microcosm.Pub/GhoulsRule
EU Safety Information: microcosmpublishing.com/gpsr

To join the ranks of high-class stores that feature Microcosm titles, talk to your rep: In the U.S. COMO (Atlantic), ABRAHAM (Midwest), sales@microcosm.pub (Texas, Oklahoma, Louisiana, Arkansas), IMPRINT (Pacific), TURNAROUND (UK, Africa, Europe, Middle East), UTP/MANDA (Canada), NEWSOUTH (Australia/New Zealand), Sendpoints (Asia), HarperCollins (India), and FAIRE in the gift trade.

Did you know that you can buy our books directly from us at sliding scale rates? Support a small, independent publisher and pay less than Amazon's price at **www.Microcosm.Pub.**

Global labor conditions are bad, and our roots in industrial Cleveland in the '70s and '80s made us appreciate the need to treat workers right. Therefore, our books are MADE IN THE USA.

Microcosm's workers and authors are paid solely from book sales. If you downloaded this book from some sketchy part of the Internet or picked up what appears to be a bootleg, please support our hardworking team by purchasing a copy directly from us and encouraging your communities to do the same. Paying for our books and zines helps us publish work that's far better than anything AI can come up with. Additionally, a 2025 MIT study revealed that AI inhibits humanity's critical thinking ability. Since critical thinking is one of our core values, we prohibit any use of our books to "train" generative artificial "intelligence" (AI) technologies, because seriously, WTF?

Ghouls Rule

A Celebration of Female Movie Monsters

Emma Alice Johnson

CONTENTS

"To be able to fly, to be smoke, to be a wolf, to know the night and live in it forever? That's not so bad. You call us monsters, but when you dream, you dream of flying, and changing, and living without death. You envy us."

—*Rachel in Clive Barker's* Nightbreed

INTRODUCTION

I've always loved monsters. One of the best days of my life came when I was in first grade. My dad walked into my room and handed me a stack of monster movie magazines he had collected as a kid. They had titles like *Famous Monsters of Filmland*, *Fantastic Monsters of the Films*, and *Castle of Frankenstein*. I'd never seen anything like them. Yes, I'd watched horror movies with my dad, but now, here in front of me, was page after page showing full-size photos of the monsters that fleetingly skittered in the shadows across the screen, revealing them in glorious detail.

I stayed in my bedroom for days, lying on the yellow shag carpet, intoxicated by the scent of old newsprint as I flipped through these magazines, learning about how each monster was made, and what movies it appeared in. I took in every fact and fell in love with these strange creatures.

I was not scared of the monsters. I was fascinated with them. I saw myself in them.

But one thing was missing. Almost all the monsters were men.

"No one ever thinks chicks do shit like this. A girl can be a slut, tease, bitch, or the virgin next door," Ginger explains to her sister in the film *Ginger Snaps* as they bury a body in their shed. A girl can be anything but a monster. It's a flippant comment from a teenage werewolf, but it bears out when you look at the history of cinema. To this day, how many women in film fall into the above categories? And more importantly, where are all the monstrous women?

Before exploring that question, let's address this one: What is a monster? Merriam-Webster offers the best dictionary definition I could find: "an animal of strange or terrifying shape." By that definition, however, a platypus is a monster. If a platypus showed up in your bed one night and chased you around your house, then perhaps you would agree that a platypus is a monster. For the purposes of this book though, I'm going to be a bit more rigid in my definition.

To me, a monster must not only be of "strange or

terrifying shape," but there must also be an element of myth, science, or the supernatural. This expanded definition includes the typical vampires, werewolves, zombies, and frankensteins, but excludes slashers, serial killers, and cannibals. The latter may colloquially be referred to as monsters and are the subject of many horror films, but they're just regular, boring humans behaving badly. The world is full of them.

Also, aliens aren't monsters. Although they have often been used as monsters, like in the 1979 movie *Alien*, they have no inherent strangeness or terrifying-ness unless they are taken out of their natural context, like the platypus in your bed. In *Star Wars*, the Mos Eisley cantina is filled with aliens that look wild and diverse to our eyes, but they are an ordinary part of life for Luke Skywalker.

That is not to say monsters are solely the domain of horror. They are also present in science fiction, fantasy, and more. Monster movies frequently blend genres, and in a sense, are a genre all their own.

With all this cinematic history in mind, what image do you think of first when you envision a monster? When you picture a vampire, a werewolf, or a zombie, is it a man or a woman? For that matter, how many female monsters can you name off the top of your head?

Don't be ashamed if it's only a handful. Looking at the first 150 issues of *Famous Monsters of Filmland*, which originally ran from 1958 to 1983 and served as the go-to publication about these films, women monsters only made the cover eight times. Lon Chaney, Vincent Price, and TV horror host Zacherley made the cover two times each before the Bride of Frankenstein first appeared on the cover of issue 17. She would appear on the cover 3 more times. The magazine is only partly to blame. It was at least trying to represent the glamour ghouls, but there simply weren't many to represent at the time.

Fangoria, which took the monster movie magazine baton from *Famous Monsters* and ran with it through much of the 80s and 90s, didn't have the same excuse. Horror was booming and more monstrous women were stealing the screen, but they weren't showing up on the covers. I remember how excited I was to find issue 127 on a bookstore magazine rack in the early 90s, with its full-color photo of zombified Julie from *Return of the Living Dead 3*, marking one of the rare cover appearances of a femme monster. I stood there and read the whole article immediately.

In a genre historically dominated by men, it seems like the thought of a female monster rarely crossed anyone's mind. However, some of the earliest monsters known to humankind are female. Greek mythology brought us harpies, sirens, and gorgons. To this day, the names of these creatures are used to slander women. In antiquity, female monsters represented the worst of women, or what their male creators supposed the worst in women to be. Hideous and outwardly repulsive at first, the monster ladies eventually evolved to be more traditionally femme, hiding their monstrous traits under a veneer of beauty.

While the female monsters of Greek mythology are

the most well-known in the western world, monstrous femmes can be found in the myths and folk tales of nearly all cultures. For example, stories of vagina dentata, women with sharp teeth in their vaginas, exist across the globe.

Later, female monsters occasionally appeared in theater, such as the witches in Shakespeare's *Macbeth*, as well as in fiction, often as vampires. A notable entry in the lady vampire genre is *Carmilla*, the 1872 novella by Irish author Sheridan Le Fanu, which predated the more well-known *Dracula* by Bram Stoker. The latter features its own group of bloodsucking ladies. Dracula's gals, Carmilla, and many other lady monsters from fiction and theater would eventually find their way to the screen in adaptations.

In the early days of film, monstrous femmes served primarily as background characters. In 1896's *House of the Devil* by Georges Méliès, often considered the first horror film, a parade of various spooks includes a gaggle of white-cloaked, big-nosed witches who chase a pair of soldiers around a castle. Another witch appears in 1898's *A Cavalier's Dream*, existing mainly to harass the titular character while he tries to eat.

In 1906's *The Witch*, again by Georges Méliès, the witch gets a bit more screentime. Her name is Carabosse and she is the epitome of witchiness, with her hooked nose and pointy black hat. She even flies across the moonlit sky on her broom. Though only a 12-minute short film, this entry was the first instance of a female monster being the title character. Unfortunately, it didn't become common practice. The next instance was in 1925's short

The Gorgon's Head, though I'm not sure it gets full credit. It's only the monstrous femme's head for which the film is titled, after all. This is also the first of several films that tell the Greek myth of Medusa, which I'll cover in more depth later in this book.

When it comes to feature-length films, *The Bride of Frankenstein* was the first monstrous femme to be the star of the show. Sort of. She only appears onscreen for a matter of minutes. However, she made an immense impact, judging by the number of films that have expanded on her story, the volume of critical essays about her, and, of course, all those *Famous Monsters of Filmland* covers.

So why are there so few female monsters? Is it the patriarchy's fault? Is it the result of so few women being involved in the making of monster movies? Is it a reluctance to show women as anything other than beautiful, anything other than the damsel in distress?

Likely, a little bit of each is true.

Perhaps the answer to the question lies in what monsters represent. Monsters are rarely the bad guys. While monsters may commit harmful acts, they tend to be portrayed as a victim-hero, and often those acts are justified to an extent. Frankenstein's monster was haphazardly created and then venomously discarded by his creator, let loose to be ostracized by humankind. Was killing his creator's family that much of an overreaction? I'm not sure I would have done it differently, though Medusa did. When she was cursed with her head of snakes that turn men into stone, she didn't go on a statue-making spree.

She went to live a solitary life, but dudes kept coming to harass her.

While it may not be easy to see Medusa, Frankenstein's monster, his bride, and similar characters as heroes in the traditional sense, they are certainly the characters that most resonate with people. You've likely seen a Medusa tattoo on someone. Have you ever seen a Perseus tattoo? Probably not. T-shirts featuring the Bride of Frankenstein outnumber those featuring Dr. Frankenstein by something like a million to one (this is a non-scientific calculation). The magazine was called *Famous Monsters of Filmland*, after all, not *Famous Guys and Gals of Filmland.* It's the monsters we care about. It's the monsters we see ourselves in.

I mentioned earlier that I saw myself in the monsters I watched and read about as a kid. I have a congenital condition called Crouzon syndrome. I spent a lot of time in hospitals at a very young age getting very intense surgeries. I have vivid memories of my head wrapped in bandages like a mummy. When the bandages came off, my shaved head was covered in scars like Frankenstein. Other kids called me names, often the names of monsters from movies, because I looked different from them. So how could I not see myself in these characters?

These days I like to refer to myself as unconventionally pretty. That's more fun and positive, but I definitely did my time looking in the mirror and believing I was ugly. I don't think I'm alone either. I think nearly everyone has had a moment of seeing themselves as less than beautiful, if not totally monstrous.

But if anything, this should be reason for equal representation of females in monsterdom. We have hefty stakes in discussions like these. A survey conducted by Dove in 2010 found that only 11 percent of women worldwide would describe themselves as beautiful. Dove has a bit of a bias in selling products to make women feel beautiful, but the number is still startlingly low.

Perhaps the idea of a female monster itself is subversive. Men are expected to be strong and aggressive, which are traits that can be easily exaggerated into monstrosity. Women, on the other hand, are expected to be pretty, to be polite and nurturing. Monstrous women are in direct opposition to those expectations. That we can be monstrous—ugly, strong, aggressive, mean—and yet still be female, challenges stereotypes and gives us new power.

Or am I reading too much meaning into all this?

It would be easy to say, "Hey, we love monsters because they're neat! They look wild! They, by their nature, require wild stories and that's fun!" But that wouldn't make much of a book, nor would it be true. I may have fallen in love with monsters because of how superficially cool they are, but that's not why I'm still watching monster movies now that I am a so-called grownup.

When researching this book, I stumbled on a social media post from a young film fan asking why *The Bride of Frankenstein* is considered a feminist classic. I was surprised to see response after response raging about how this is simply a monster movie, with no deeper meaning at all. The idea that a work borne of Mary Shelley's implicitly meaning-rich novel, a work made by a gay director during a time period when gay people were less accepted than they are today, would have no meaning beyond monsters is bonkers to me. Further, the willful objection to finding meaning in works seems so maliciously anti-intellectual it borders on villainous. It's Oz begging you not to look behind the curtain, to believe only the surface-level presentation when there is so much else there to discover.

This isn't to say I think you need to always look for meaning in movies, or any other art for that matter. I love enjoying art at a purely aesthetic, surface level. Renowned activist and critic Susan Sontag wrote an essay called "Against Interpretation." In it, she argues "interpretation amounts to the philistine refusal to leave the work of art alone." She calls interpretation . . .

> "the revenge of the intellect upon the world. To interpret is to impoverish, to deplete the world—in order to set up a shadow world of 'meanings.' It is to turn the world into this world. ('This world'! As if there were any other.)"

In other words, to interpret is to take a beautiful thing and say it is not good enough on its own and it can only be good if one can find some meaning within it.

I think it's true that we can become so obsessed with finding meaning in a work of art that we overlook all that is beautiful on the surface, and we risk throwing the artist away and inserting ourselves instead. At the same time, I don't think there's any reason why we cannot do both. Our brains are complex enough that we can visit and revisit a work and look at it with a different intent every time.

You can watch *The She-Creature* and be awed by the monster. What a brilliant creation! You can ask, "Who came up with that and how did they construct it?" You can love the very surface with all your heart. This is usually how a film imprints itself on me, and there is nothing less about loving a film this way, regardless of what your English lit teacher may have impressed upon you. A thing can be a thing and you can love it as such.

Then you can watch *The She-Creature* a second time, and you can think, "Oh, this film is about a woman standing up to domestic abuse!" Then a third time, you can think about how all the men in the movie are absolutely useless fools. You might ask, "What were the men who created the movie thinking in presenting their gender this way? Were they thinking at all?"

Then you can go back a fourth time and say, "The beach and ocean footage is so lovely, and the effect of the monster emerging from the ocean is so iconic I should get it tattooed on my arm."

All ways of watching have value. One does not take away from the other.

It's odd to claim a work of art doesn't have meaning. Art isn't made in a vacuum. Sure, a filmmaker may not have intended a film to have a certain meaning, but maybe they inserted it subconsciously. I doubt Jackie Kong, when making *Blood Diner*, intentionally said, "Sheetar should only kill men, but nonetheless Sheetar only kills men and that feels meaningful in and of itself," if only in the fleeting thought, "As a woman, I do not need to be scared of this monster. I am not this monster's target."

Films are made in a certain time and place, and that adds meaning as well. I love *Godzilla* films on the surface level, but it can't be written off as a coincidence that they arose in the wake of the atomic bomb hitting Japan. Nor was it coincidence that, in the U.S., the Universal Monster films brought about a surge in monster fandom during the Great Depression. David J. Skal's book *The Monster Show: A Cultural History of Horror* covers how the monsters that scare us are tied to the times from which they are born, how they are often avatars for larger societal fears, like the financial hardships of the depression, the pain of the atomic bomb, and more.

Even if a film doesn't have a meaning imbued intentionally or unintentionally by the filmmaker, and it doesn't have any particular historical or cultural meaning, it can still have a personal meaning for each person watching it. We all create our own personal meanings for the films we watch, sometimes intentionally, but mostly unconsciously. *Star Wars* has meaning to me because it was the only VHS in the hospital when I was recovering from surgery as a child, and I escaped into it every day to take me away from the pain. To erase that and say *Star Wars* is just about space people and laser swords would be to erase my own history.

Even claiming a film has no meaning beyond being a monstrous romp is in itself granting it a meaning of your own creation. You are saying, "This is what this work means to me because this is what I need from this work. I need for it to be something I can escape to, and if I'm thinking about it, I'm thinking about the acting, or the sets, or the glorious monster makeup that made the characters iconic, not feminism! I don't want no stinking feminism, not from *The Bride of Frankenstein*!"

And if that surface-level enjoyment is all you want, bless you, and I have tried to speak to that as well, because I love that too. But I also love connecting dots, and in many of these works, *The Bride of Frankenstein* included, they are not difficult to connect.

With this book, I want to celebrate lady monsters and the women who have portrayed them, from the most well-known like the Bride, to the most obscure. I want to explore their histories, their creation and, yes, even their meaning, where appropriate, because often their stories are our stories.

I want you to flip through these pages with the same joy I felt when I was first given those old monster magazines. If you are new to monster movies, I hope this book can get you excited about the genre and provide a roadmap for your explorations. If you are a long-timer like me, I promise you will discover something you didn't know about these movies, whether it's a new way of looking at them or an interesting fact about how they were made.

Let the celebration begin!

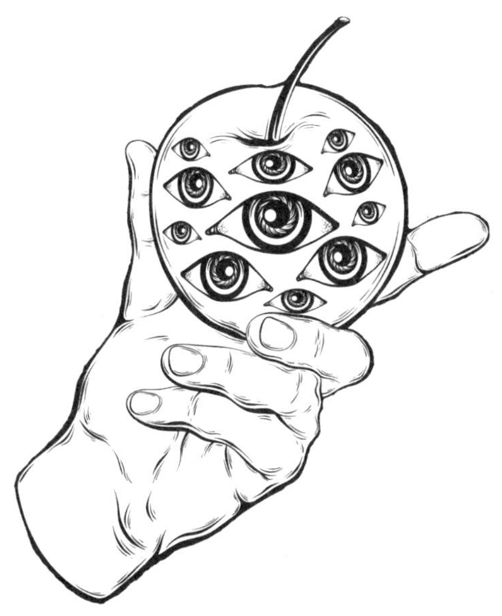

THE ORIGINAL WOMAN

"She comes from the beginning of time, huge and indestructible, and I'm the force that gives her life." So says hypnotist Dr. Carlo Lombardi, describing the eponymous monster of 1956's *The She-Creature*. He's right about the first part and wrong about the second, though he doesn't know it at first.

The She-Creature is the manifestation of an emotionally and psychologically abused woman's past self. How far past? She's prehistoric, the first life body of the woman to crawl out of the depths of the ocean. She's a humanoid, fishlike brute covered with scales and spikes and . . . strangely beautiful blonde hair. Just to make it clear that, prehistoric or not, she's all woman, she's also equipped with massive breasts. And she's here to kill anyone who gets in her way.

Marla English stars as Andrea Talbott, a carnival follower who has fallen in with Carlo, serving reluctantly as his assistant and hypnosis subject as he obsesses over her. The film begins as their act, which has up till now been relegated to the carnival sideshow, has caught the attention of the wealthy elite in an unnamed seaside town. The wives are obsessed and convinced, while the husbands, primarily businessman Timothy Chappel, are skeptical but eager to exploit the doctor and his assistant to make a buck or two.

In his shows, Carlo uses hypnosis to regress Andrea back to her life from 300 years ago, in which she has an English accent and knows the names of kings. When nobody is looking, he regresses her further and further, putting her in a deep enough hypnosis that not only does she connect with her original self, her original self manifests physically, emerging from the ocean nearby to go on killing sprees, all while Andrea's human form remains in her hypnotic state. Of course, Carlo "predicts" the murders ancient Andrea, the She-Creature, commits each time she appears, increasing his celebrity status (and sales of his book).

Dr. Ted Erickson is the would-be hero of the story, having been dragged into this social scene while dating

Chappel's daughter, Dorothy. Ted is a so-called legitimate hypnotist who wants to expose Carlo as a charlatan. His failed attempts to do so only increase the stock in Carlo.

In Ted's quest to break Carlo's hold over Andrea, he too becomes obsessed with the woman. He leaves Dorothy behind to her wealthy social life, spending more and more time with the hypnotist's assistant. She falls for him in the process, and begins to fight harder against the hold Carlo has on her. She eventually works up the nerve to tell Carlo, "Someday I'm going to kill you." He replies, "I should kill you, Andrea, but the artist is vain. He can't destroy the beauty he's created." He becomes more and more possessive, while risking putting Andrea in deeper and deeper hypnotic states.

The film culminates in one final show. Once again, Andrea is put into deep hypnosis and the She-Creature is manifested. Carlo tries to exert control, to get her to kill Ted. But at the last moment she pulls back and instead finally resists Carlo, killing him while he stands over her hypnotised human form, still trying to control her till the very end. The police arrive and the She-Creature is chased back to the ocean, where she disappears into history, and Andrea's human form reawakens.

For star Marla English, this film comes near the end of a whirlwind 5-year Hollywood career that began in 1952, after she won a San Diego beauty pageant. Still in her late teens, she started with bit parts before being promoted to bigger roles in B-movies. She easily bounced between genres, owning the screen in crime, western, and war movies, as well as sci-fi and horror. Narrowly missing a chance at fame after opting out of co-starring in a Spencer Tracy flick, she left acting as she entered her 20s. Preferring to stay out of the limelight, she rarely gave interviews, so little is known about what she did next. Onscreen though, her characters ranged from cutthroat criminals to supportive wives. Her depiction of Andrea Talbott in *The She-Creature* is among her meekest characters, at least in human form.

Despite the surface story of greed and hypnotism, more than anything else, this film is about domestic abuse. It's not even an allegory, as this theme is overt. Carlo is a narcissist who, despite his claims to love Andrea, is primarily interested in controlling her. He treats her like a possession, saying she belongs to him and can never leave. One minute he makes a statement like, "You can never leave me." When she tries to resist, he suddenly becomes a caring poet: "You're the light that shines in the darkness." He lays it on thick. He's a classic manipulator.

Andrea is his meal ticket, so of course he would never voluntarily let her leave. He likely believes it when he tells the police officer at the start of the film that he is the force giving the She-Creature life, but he is wrong. He may put Andrea under hypnosis, but it is entirely her who brings her past life self into the physical reality of the present. In the end, she finally realizes this, and she brings her strength to bear to kill her abuser.

Despite other characters bopping around here and there, this is almost purely a battle of wills between

Andrea and Carlo. There are no men coming to save her. The police are worthless. The scientists called in to debunk the hypnotist are equally so. The rich men capitalizing on him have no interest in stopping anything, and as they act high and mighty over their wives who believe in hypnotism, it is the wives who are right, not them.

Ted, the man who appears to be the hero based on the amount of screen time he's given, has nothing to offer but baffled expressions and half-hearted pep talks for Andrea. No, layers of male bluster notwithstanding, it is Andrea, in her manifestation as the She-Creature, who finally breaks Carlo's spell and bashes him to death with her lobster-y claws, as Ted stands by simpering.

I'm fascinated with the idea that the She-Creature is the first life body of Andrea. What is unspoken in the film is that, if she is one woman's first ancestor, then she must also be the ancestor of all women, a scaly Eve from which we all eventually sprang. Of course, we know humans didn't evolve from prehistoric fish women (although if anyone wants to start that church, count on seeing me at Sunday service).

Maybe we aren't meant to take her as our literal antecedent though. After all, the movie seems to make a point of ignoring any men that may be in the lineage from the She-Creature to the current world's Andrea. Maybe she is not literally the first woman in a genealogical sense, but the manifestation of everything primordial stored in all women. Or maybe she's the manifestation of all the anger accumulated from centuries of emotional, mental and physical abuse, of all the accumulated anger not only from Andrea, but from all women, pulled forward in time to take revenge on everything that has been done to her daughters and granddaughters.

Okay, okay, maybe she's just a prehistoric fish lady. But a cooler prehistoric fish lady has never been seen on film before or since. The She-Creature was brought to life by the husband-and-wife team of Paul and Jackie Blaisdell. While Paul designed the creature and often gets sole credit, the two were truly a team who worked together on all their projects, as explained in Randy Palmer's exhaustive career overview, *Paul Blaisdell, Monster Maker.*

If you close your eyes and envision monsters from 50s and 60s B-movies, it's likely Blaisdell monsters you're envisioning. On miniscule budgets, the duo came up with wildly creative creatures, and the She-Creature costume, which Paul nicknamed Cuddles, is widely regarded as their best. Creature creation has a long history as a DIY endeavor, going back to all the complex techniques Lon Chaney used to bring his horror characters to life in the silent days of the cinema. The Blaisdells took DIY to a new level though, working on budgets as low as a couple hundred dollars, which was a pittance even in 50s money.

Paul didn't have any experience in special effects when he got his first job. He built models as a hobby, but he also wrote and illustrated science fiction stories. It was through that work that he eventually connected to folks in the world of B-movies, who hired him because nobody else wanted to work for the low rates they were offering.

Working out of their garage, the Blaisdells spent eight weeks building the She-Creature costume. They started with a simple pair of long johns, using them as the foundation on which they added scales made of foam rubber, stomach claws carved out of pinewood, and more. They weren't above using store-bought items either. The She-Creature's fangs were a modified set of novelty store fangs. Much of the costume's greatness didn't make it to the final film, such as a tail that could swipe back and forth, in part because of the rush job that was filming the low-budget picture. The massive breasts were not on the initial costume design, but made out of block foam and added later at the request of director Edward L. Cahn. Like he did in most of his films, Paul operated the suit himself.

Considering the subject of reincarnation in this film, it's only fitting that the She-Creature was reincarnated in a number of other films after this. With some modifications, the costume was also used in *Voodoo Woman* (1957), *The Ghost of Drag Strip Hollow* (1959), and more.

I like to think that, despite the plots of these latter films, despite the actions of the characters, it is the She-Creature manifesting in unusual places. When the doctor teams up with the voodoo priest to turn a woman into the Voodoo Woman, maybe what he has actually done is put her under deep hypnosis and accidentally summoned the original woman, like Carlo did with Andrea. Maybe she will be pulled into whatever film reality, or any reality for that matter, that needs her to do some indiscriminate skull-mashing. Maybe she will rise again from the ocean, whenever women need her.

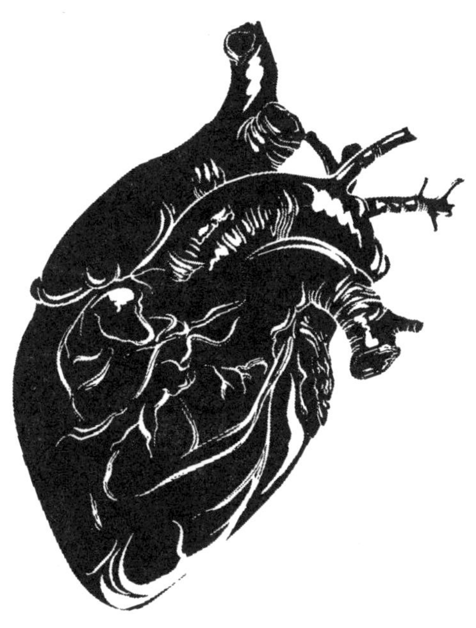

THE MANY BRIDES OF FRANKENSTEIN

Mary Shelley's *Frankenstein* is recognized today as one of the greatest monster stories ever created. Initially published anonymously in 1818 to critical disdain over its perceived lack of a moral, the novel nonetheless caught the popular imagination, and this story about creation has led to the creation of hundreds of legitimate and illegitimate remakes, sequels, riffs and more.

On its surface, this book about men creating men wouldn't seem to have much to say about women.

Presuming so is a mistake. Shelley was the daughter of Mary Wollstonecraft, regarded as one of the first feminist philosophers. Wollstonecraft died days after Shelley's birth, but her daughter spent time with her mother's writings before beginning her own writing career, and it shows. Literary critic Elizabeth Young calls *Frankenstein* "one of the proof-texts for contemporary feminist literary criticism." *Frankenstein* has much to say about womanhood for those willing to look, and what it says has been reaffirmed and even expanded upon every time the story is recreated.

In her essay " 'My Hideous Progeny': The Lady and the Monster," feminist literary critic Mary Poovey explains how Victor Frankenstein's goal in bringing his creature to life is not benevolent, as the character first alludes, but self-serving. He wants to create a "new species" that would be thankful to him to the point of worship. He says, "No father could claim the gratitude of his child so completely as I should deserve theirs." In bringing his creation to life, he circumvents relationships and women entirely, to make a child that is solely of man. He would, as Poovey puts it, "reduce all domestic ties to those that center on and feed his selfish desires."

The Bride of Frankenstein does not appear in the novel, at least not in completed form. She is, however, an important part of the story. Despite his initial musings at the outset, once Frankenstein has completed his monster, he is horrified by what he has done. He abandons both his project and his creation, along with his dreams of being the father to a new species.

Frankenstein's monster retreats into the world, only to find the world hates him for looking different. After years of roaming and failing to find a place where he can be accepted, he returns to find his creator. He begs his creator to make a woman, someone as horrific as him, who, in their shared hideousness and ostracization, would be forced into a bond, then run away together to the furthest reaches of the Earth, never to see another human again.

With pity, and not much remorse, Frankenstein agrees. Of course, it is not an overnight process, and he does not exactly remember how he brought his creature to life. He goes off on an adventure to gather knowledge and equipment, ending up in a run-down cottage on a barely inhabited island. He toils and begins building a woman for his monster.

Halfway through the process, he changes his mind. The thought of being the father of a new species has now turned sour to him. He imagines his two creatures creating a race of devils that would destroy humanity. Never mind that his creature's only malicious acts at this point have been limited to targeting his creator and his creator's family. Still, in his fit of feigned magnanimity, Frankenstein destroys the half-built woman, scattering her mismatched pieces around the cabin. His creature appears, having followed him here, begging him to reconsider. Frankenstein refuses.

1935's *The Bride of Frankenstein* fulfills the promise the doctor made to the creature, and in a sense, the promise

Shelley made to her readers. This was the first film to explore this idea of a female creature, but it would not be the last. This, the first of many sequels to 1931's *Frankenstein*, picks up right where the first movie left off.

Before it does though, there is a prelude. Lord Byron, Percy Shelley, and Mary Shelley, the author of Frankenstein, have gathered on a dark and stormy night. Byron marvels that someone so beautiful could write such a horrifying tale.

"She is an angel," Byron proclaims.

Mary replies, with the slightest touch of sarcasm in her voice and a hint of a smirk on her face, "You think so."

Then she continues her tale. Both Dr. Frankenstein and his monster have survived the fire set for them by the mob of townspeople at the end of the first movie. Frankenstein, seriously injured, returns to his castle, where his fiancé, Elizabeth, awaits. The monster goes into hiding.

In his sickbed, Frankenstein muses about what he's done, and not entirely regretfully. He's soon visited by a Dr. Pretorius, who shares the desire to play god. Pretorius lacks even the weak voice of reason Frankenstein is constantly fighting.

Pretorius says, "Sometimes I have wondered if life wouldn't be much more amusing if we were all devils, and no nonsense about angels and being good."

Pretorius sees Frankenstein's dream as shortsighted. Giving life to one man? That is barely godlike. Better to also give life to a woman for that man to mate with, to watch them multiply and create an entire manmade race to populate the earth. That is the ultimate in playing god.

Despite being quite interested, Frankenstein listens to his voice of reason and refuses to join Pretorius in this quest. But Pretorius befriends Frankenstein's rogue monster, who has learned much in his travels, including speech. With the promise of a mate, the monster kidnaps Frankenstein's fiancé, Elizabeth, holding her hostage until Frankenstein creates a Bride for him.

Frankenstein begins his task, and what little ethics he and Pretorius may have had go to the wayside in their shared fervor for their project. Dead bodies are stolen, but the acquired heart is no good. They need a fresh one. They charge one of their unscrupulous assistants to acquire it, promising him money. Of course, he does get a fresh one, murdering its owner in the process. With this final piece and Pretorius's lab-grown brain, the two men masquerading as gods harness lightning and bring their Bride to life.

Wrapped in bandages and draped in a hospital sheet in a mockery of a wedding dress, with a white-streaked tower of a beehive hairdo, the Bride is a sewn together collection of dead body parts, made for the sole purpose of being a mate to Frankenstein's monster.

She has other ideas though.

Scared, twitching, and off-balance, she takes in her surroundings. Her would-be husband is brought in. When he touches her, she screams. He freaks out, crashing into the machinery, which goes haywire. As the lab starts to blow up, the monster allows Frankenstein and his fiancé to escape but keeps his Bride back. "We belong dead," he says.

With only three screaming minutes of screentime, the Bride became the most iconic female monster in the history of film. Some have argued it's because of her memorable look, from her lightning-struck beehive hairdo to her makeup to her sheet-and-bandage wedding gown.

The Bride's hair and makeup were designed by Jack Pierce, who based them on another iconic woman: Nefertiti. A bust of that woman of Egyptian royalty had been discovered a couple decades earlier, in 1912, though archeologists date it back to 1345 BC.

It's not really the hair and makeup that makes the Bride iconic though, is it? It's her scream, and everything it represents.

From the moment the idea of creating a woman is introduced, her male makers take it as a given that she will happily be a wife and mother. The contrary never crosses their mind through all their scheming. Even knowing their monster man has gone rogue, they do not ponder for a second that this woman will be anything other than docile. Of course, they are very wrong.

Her perfect screaming rejection of all that was and is expected of a woman is what makes her iconic. She awakens to a world where she is being told this is all she has to look forward to, and she says no in the fiercest, clearest way any woman has ever said no to all of this before or since.

This is the scream I want to scream whenever I'm asked

if I'll ever get married or have kids, when that question is floated as if that's my raison dêtre, and no thought has been given to the possibility that I would want something else. And here it is, a hundred years since, feminism with a solid foothold, and still these are questions women are asked. Can you imagine how cathartic the Bride's scream must have felt for women in 1935?

Then I think, maybe it's not just about the expectation of a woman to be a wife and mother, but also the expectation men have about what they can take from a woman. I think about the way Frankenstein's monster touches this woman, who has just woken up, and keeps touching her even as she screams. And I think about the way I screamed when I woke up in a darkened room one night to a man touching me without my permission, and how many other women have experienced that exact same moment, and how the Bride's scream must live in the ether, waiting to come out of the mouth of any woman who needs it.

Elsa Lanchester, the actress who portrays the Bride, pulled inspiration for that scream from a strange source. In an interview on *The Dick Cavett Show*, she describes the scream as being like an angry swan, not just the sound, but the physicality, the way she moves her head. Not the traditional acting method for sure, but nothing about Lanchester's life was traditional.

Her rollicking career began in cabaret and theater. She moved into film after marrying the actor Charles Laughton, who she often appeared with onscreen. She appeared in over 60 films across as many years, including *Mary Poppins*, *That*

Darn Cat, and *Willard*, as well as winning a Golden Globe for best supporting actress in *Witness for the Prosecution*. Her roles were incredibly diverse, and she only returned to the horror genre toward the end of her career with parts in films like *Willard* and *Terror in the Wax Museum*.

My favorite part of Lanchester's career, aside from her role in *The Bride of Frankenstein*, is her music. Before she began acting, she had a nightclub act performing old Victorian songs. She continued to pursue music in parallel to her film career, eventually releasing a trio of albums in the 1950s: *Songs for a Shuttered Parlor*, *Songs for a Smoke-Filled Room*, and *Cockney London*. In her husband's intro to one of these albums, he describes her act: "She wore, of all things, a pink paper skirt, a blue bodice, her long and witty legs, her mop of unruly red hair, and a men's high silk hat to top it all."

Her songs are saucy and filled with double entendre. Titles like "If You Peek in My Gazebo" are not, in fact, about peeking into a gazebo. Lanchester delivers them with a wink and a nudge, her voice undisciplined and warbling, often more talking than singing, sometimes coy, sometimes breathy, sometimes sounding a few whiskeys deep, sometimes outright shouting or laughing, sometimes randomly rolling her Rs for no clear reason, all over wild piano plinking.

A highlight is "Never Go Walking without Your Hat Pin." Here she retells self-defense advice given to her by her grandmother about bringing a hat pin with you when you go out. She sings, "It's about the best protection that you've got" and "the law won't let you carry more than that."

The Bride is defenseless at the conclusion of the film, unfortunately. "We belong dead," Frankenstein's monster says before killing himself and the Bride. It seems poetic on the surface, but he offers her no choice. Her life is crushed out because she will not allow herself to be taken by this man she doesn't know, and this man thinks if he can't have her, nobody will. It's truly terrifying.

The Bride of Frankenstein is regarded as one of, if not the greatest, horror films of all time. In addition to its heady swirl of themes—like playing god, concepts of a master race, women rejecting their place, and more—it is also one of the first examples of a horror comedy, veering from satire to slapstick to seriousness in a manner so graceful it's hardly been replicated since.

In a genre where characters are twisted every which way, put through the ringer to make an extra buck until they are completely used up, it's a miracle the Bride never returned in the many Universal Monsters Frankenstein movies that came after it. Lanchester would have been up for a return though. "It would be very interesting to do an elderly bride," she said in a late-career interview with the magazine *Monsters of the Movies.* She had a unique vision for the comeback: "When she was dragged out of her grave, time had had its way with her, like other corpses."

Instead of an official return to the screen, the Bride's presence has been limited to similar characters in the various remakes and reimaginings that have rained down over the years. Perhaps that scarcity has helped her hold her iconic status.

However, in the various reimaginings, we get to see a fuller story play out. In the same way *The Bride of Frankenstein* fulfilled the original novel's promise of the creation of a female monster, movies like *Frankenhooker*, *Blood Diner*, and *Patchwork* allow us to see what might have happened if the Bride had been allowed to live. What would she have done with her life?

Before we get to the answer to that question though, we have to follow how the theme of the original novel expands or, more accurately, mutates in the years following the release of *The Bride of Frankenstein.* After all, a story about a man creating a man is one thing. A story about a man creating a woman is another thing entirely. The motives of the male creators veer from sheer desire to create life, to a desire to create a perfect object, to a desire to create a perfect object they can own.

The latter is implied in *The Bride of Frankenstein* in how the Bride's creators simply expect their female creation will happily go along with the life of wifery and motherhood they have created her for. But in *Frankenstein's Daughter* (1958), the creator, the grandchild of Victor Frankenstein, says the quiet part out loud. He exclaims that a woman's brain is ideal for his creation, as they are naturally submissive. This doctor is comically misogynist in his treatment of women throughout the film, so he deserves everything he gets when it turns out he's wrong and his female creation goes on a rampage.

(*Frankenstein's Daughter* is not the ideal example. The special effects team didn't get the memo that the monster was supposed to be a woman. Their budget wouldn't allow them to recreate the special effects makeup, so they smeared lipstick on the giant man's Frankenface and made sure the characters gendered her properly. Good enough!)

So the idea of a woman's brain as being submissive is proven wrong time and time again, but that doesn't stop the various doctors from leaning into the project of creating a perfect physical body. 1944's *House of Frankenstein* is the first film to introduce the idea of using the frankensteining technology, for lack of a better term, to perfect someone.

Here, Gustav Niemann, a doctor trying to recreate Frankenstein's techniques, promises a hunchback, Daniel, that he will put his brain in a perfect body. He doesn't, and the plot devolves into a mishmash of schemes to put different brains in different bodies for different reasons, but it's the first to move from the idea of the original Frankenstein theme of creating a new being to creating a perfect body for an existing being, which is the dominant idea in the rest of the films discussed.

The Revenge of Frankenstein (1958) builds on this theme a little more, with Frankenstein returning to follow through on the promise to the hunchback, giving him a handsome body.

Leave it to B-movies though to speak the truth of the desire to create a perfect body. The real value of this power to men is not to create perfect bodies for other men, but to do so for women that they can then make their own. Of course, like the Bride, the women have different ideas.

In *The Brain That Wouldn't Die* (1962), Dr. Bill Cortner and Jan, his fiancée, played by Virginia Leith, get in a serious car crash on the way to an outing at their cabin. Jan's head is severed. Thankfully, Cortner has been working on some unorthodox transplant operations, and this gives him a chance to try them out. He preserves Jan's head. Bandaged like the Bride of Frankenstein, she soaks in a shallow pan filled with serum, tubes, and wires coiling to and from her disembodied head, while she awaits a replacement bod.

It doesn't take Cortner long to turn his search into a lecherous hunt for his idea of the perfect body, which means haunting burlesque shows and beauty pageants, even driving around neighborhoods like an absolute creep and staring at women walking around. Every time he finds a target and gets her alone, someone else shows up to unknowingly save the day.

Of course, Jan doesn't consent to any of this. "Let me die," she screams repeatedly, heartbreakingly. She doesn't want to be rebuilt. She does not want any of what Cortner is planning. She hates her new life. "Like all quantities," she says, "horror has its ultimate, and I'm that."

Cortner continues his quest to find a body, leaving the woman he claims to love sitting alone in her shallow tub of serum. He turns to an ex-girlfriend, a figure model who poses nude for private photo sessions. She has a facial scar, and he promises to fix it for her. He doesn't mention that his fix entails cutting her head off and putting his current gal's head on instead.

But while he's off searching for a new body, Jan finds one of her own, in a sense. As a side effect of the life-preserving serum, she has developed a psychic connection to the doctor's previous experiment, a mishmashed body of limbs locked in a nearby closet. She encourages this creature to break out, and he does. He kills the doctor before Jan's transplant operation can be completed.

In the skirmish, the lab starts on fire, mirroring the fire at the conclusion of *The Bride of Frankenstein*, but here Jan wants to die. The closet monster saves Cortner's ex and escapes, while the flames engulf Jan and she laughs a laugh that, in a perfect world, would be as iconic as our Bride's scream. It's a laugh of rejecting the plan a man has set out for her.

Interestingly, *The Brain that Wouldn't Die* had a twin film. Though *The Head* made it to release in the U.S. a year earlier in 1961, both were produced at the same time, *The Head* in Germany and *The Brain that Wouldn't Die* in the U.S. Like *TBTWD*, *The Head* features a scientist committed to transplanting a woman's head onto a more beautiful body. In *The Head* though, the woman's head is still attached to her own body, but it is hunchbacked.

The woman, Irene, goes along with the idea of being cured of her back ailment, though the doctor doesn't tell her how he plans to do it. Like Cortner in *TBTWD*, this doctor also haunts strip clubs to find a body, choosing a stripper named Lilly. Unlike Cortner, this doctor finishes what he started. This doesn't lead Irene to go on a monster-like killing spree though. It brings her existential angst.

"What is my past?" she asks. "The past of Lilly's body or the past of my head?"

While the concept of killing people to get body parts goes back to *The Bride of Frankenstein*, when unbeknownst to the creator, his henchmen kills a random woman to get a heart, these two twin films were the first to introduce the concept of killing sex workers. This is important for a couple reasons. First, there's the implication that sex workers' bodies are more desirable, though their minds are not of value. Second, there's the implication that their lives are lesser, making their murder somehow a more acceptable crime in the eyes of their murderers.

The latter is more than an implication in 1990's *Frankenhooker*, when our mad doctor states outright that the prostitutes he plans to kill sell their bodies all the time, so what's the big deal? "If I need female body parts, I'll buy female body parts. There's a place across the river where there's thousands of women anxious to sell their parts, no questions asked!"

In *Frankenhooker*, Elizabeth Shelley, played by Patty Mullen, is living a nice suburban New Jersey life, proudly supporting her boyfriend, Jeffrey Franken, as he works on all manner of weird inventions in his mom's garage. Unfortunately, his inventions are always a little off, including the automatic lawnmower that goes awry and chops Elizabeth into pieces.

Jeffrey collects her head and a few other salvageable pieces, and tries to come up with a way to bring his love back to life. He invents an estrogen-based blood serum that will do the trick. Without all her parts though, he's forced to bring in some ringers. He crosses the river into New York City and kills a bunch of prostitutes with super-crack that causes them to explode. Taking the best parts from each of them, he builds a new body for Elizabeth and brings her back to life one stormy night.

Alas, despite Elizabeth's head on the body, the prostitutes take control. She shoves Jeffrey out of the way to go on a rampage through NYC, her body parts' memories leading the way. It's like when Irene in *The Head* asks whose memories she has, her head's or her body's. The memories of Elizabeth's new body parts are in charge now, looking for dates and dispatching men along the way.

Before *Frankenhooker*, Patty Mullen, who had been *Penthouse*'s Pet of the Year in 1988, had only one other film under her belt, but she shows a range beyond that of big, mainstream movies as she veers from meek suburban girlfriend to aggressive, sewn-together sex worker.

Jeffrey tracks her down and brings her back to his garage. He gives her another jolt and finally Elizabeth's brain kicks in. At first, she is the same proud girlfriend, happy to be alive, yes, but also amazed that Jeffrey could accomplish such a feat. Then she notices with shock her pieced-together body. Before she can get all her complaints out, the pimp whose prostitutes' bodies she's made of arrives and kills Jeffrey. Thankfully though, Jeffrey left detailed instructions on how to bring someone back.

Elizabeth's memories may be front and center at this point, but they are not alone. At the start of the film, she was submissive, doting on Jeffrey. She's stronger now, perhaps because of the new memories that come with her new body, or simply from living through this ordeal. When the pimp kills Jeffrey, her bringing him back to life is less an act of charity and more an act of revenge: his estrogen-based serum only works on female body parts, so she gives him a body to match hers, and for once, it's the doctor doing the screaming.

In *Frankenhooker*, Jeffrey immediately loses touch with the idea of bringing back Elizabeth as she was, fixating instead on making her better. In one of the most telling scenes in the movie, he shows her severed head a variety of collages with pictures of her head pasted onto the bodies of pinup models. Though Elizabeth remains unconscious through this presentation, Jeffrey has a dialogue with her imagined voice, which argues back. So subconsciously at least, he realizes he is not doing this for her, but for himself. He becomes obsessed with creating a woman with all the perfect parts, carefully measuring and inspecting the bodies of each of the prostitutes he murders, taking what he imagines is the best of each.

The theme of creating the perfect female body also drives 1987's *Blood Diner*. Unlike *Frankenhooker* and the twin head movies of the 60s though, the body created is not for a human being, but for a "bloodthirsty goddess of black magic."

Even by 80s B-movie standards, *Blood Diner* is absolutely bonkers. The film begins with two kids witnessing their uncle commit suicide-by-cop after a killing spree. Then it cuts to the kids, George and Michael, now adults, as they dig their Uncle Anwar up, chop out his brain, stuff it in a jar, and bring it back to life with a spell from an ancient book.

Anwar serves as their leader, helping them navigate the massive undertaking of creating a body for goddess Sheetar and preparing the Lumerian feast for her resurrection. Thankfully, George and Michael run a successful vegetarian diner, which is a great front for their nefarious activities. The guys start by collecting the body parts of immoral women. Well, they are immoral according to Uncle Anwar. Really, they're just gals who engage in such activities as swearing, having sex, and appearing in nude aerobics videos. None of these seem as immoral as slaughtering women, but I guess if you've got an ancient Lumerian goddess to resurrect, you have other things on your mind than tuning your moral compass.

Like Jeffrey in *Frankenhooker*, the guys piece together the best corpse bits into the perfect vessel for the goddess Sheetar, disposing of any excess meat in their special recipes and serving them to unsuspecting diners. At the same time, they are creating the meal for the Lumerian feast, the ceremony that will summon Sheetar into the body they have made, a body which is finished out by shoving Uncle Anwar's disembodied brain into the skull. So much for a body made from the bodies of immoral women. They have also, of course, kidnapped Connie, a virgin, to be the first meal for Sheetar.

The guys hold the feast in a club, feeding the crowd the

prepared food, which turns everyone into zombies. As the zombies feast, a band plays on stage. The band is led by The King of White Trash, a singer with a cartoonishly large pompadour, and features a number of members dressed as Hitlers. (As outlandish as this band is, they were a real group led by Dino Lee, who played around LA throughout the 80s.) As the band plays, Michael and George read from the ancient Lumerian text and succeed in their mission of summoning Sheetar.

Of course, Sheetar is not interested in following their plans.

Up until this point, Sheetar has been docile, serving mostly as a prop, the target of lascivious comments from Uncle Anwar. "Sheetar, your body looks good," he says. "What a set of knockers! If I only had my schlong back, you'd know the meaning of machismo." During the finale, she is clad in a ceremonial wardrobe. She has a gold cape crossed over her chest.

When she comes alive, she opens her eyes and immediately starts killing. Green ooze drools from her fanged mouth. She spreads the cape with her arms to reveal another fang-filled, vaginal mouth running vertically down her torso, chomping eagerly for her feast. She's shooting blue lasers from her fingertips. Heads are exploding.

At first, the killing seems indiscriminate. However, a closer look reveals she's only killing men. Her first victim is Uncle Anwar himself, whose personality disappears as soon as Sheetar takes over the body he and his nephews created. Did he honestly think that he, a long-dead, disembodied brain, would be able to hold his own against a bloodthirsty goddess of black magic?

At one point, Sheetar shoots a laser right over the head of a woman dancing on stage, killing one of the Hitlers instead. In fact, she completely ignores Connie, the virgin tied up in front of her, the intended first meal, even as the guys are desperately trying to feed her to Sheetar. She gobbles up George instead with her vagina maw, implying he is a virgin as well, and perhaps a tastier one. Sheetar has no loyalty to men, especially the ones who created her.

She cements her position as a mankiller in the final scene. She has snuck out of the club amidst all the chaos, and has switched her wardrobe from her Lumerian ceremonial garb to a tight red dress and matching high heels. As her heels click across the sidewalk, a man pulls up in a red convertible, saying, "Hey blondie, you look kinda nice, kinda good! Wanna come home with me tonight?" She gets in.

As the driver says one of the most cartoonishly misogynistic lines in the history of film—"Hey baby, right before I stick my big sausage in ya, what do they call ya?"—the camera turns to Sheetar. With her fangs bared, she growls, "They call me Sheetar," making it perfectly clear what is going to happen to that big sausage of his.

Originally intended to be a sequel to Herschell Gordon Lewis's cult classic, *Blood Feast*, the script was repurposed, so it's more like a reimaging with 80s sensibilities, or nonsense-ibilities, as the case may be. *Blood Diner* is one of the few cult films of the 80s directed by a woman, Jackie

Kong. In her interview in the special features for the blu-ray, she says she had three strikes against her: being a woman, Asian American, and young. Unfortunately, *Blood Diner* was the last of the only four films she made. So far, at least.

Thankfully, Sheetar was not the last of cinema's frankenwomen. 2015's *Patchwork* continues the theme of frankensteining the perfect body, though this time not for a goddess, nor for the benefit of men, but for a different purpose entirely.

Three women—Jennifer, Ellie, and Madeleine—wake up in a Los Angeles warehouse, their bodies frankensteined together into one. They were all kidnapped by unknown assailants and have no memory of what happened to them. As they try to piece together how they were pieced together, they go on a killing spree, knocking off various men who have wronged each of them, from Jennifer's married boss with whom she is having an affair, to the art bro who couldn't remember Ellie's name, to a group of frat boys who get women drunk and have sex with them on camera.

As they rampage through LA, they get to know each other. Jennifer is a high-powered business lady. Ellie is a dancer and "bar star." Madeleine turns out to be a serial killer.

They finally make their way back to the warehouse in Los Angeles where they first awoke. There they discover a rogue doctor who has been frankensteining bodies together for fun and profit. Mostly for profit. He was hired by Madeleine, who has some body image issues, to make her pretty by taking her good parts and building a new body for her with the parts of a couple other girls, who it turns out she kidnapped and killed.

Before the other two ladies in the patchwork girl can deal with that mess, they need to take on the doctor's horde of not-quite-as good creations, including owl cat. (Okay, owl cat is awesome—an adorably goofy mashup of owl and cat, two animals cute on their own made doubly so when combined. I want a whole movie about owl cat.) Thankfully the 3-in-1 have gotten good at killing and take down the horde. Except for owl cat, who seems to lack the predatory instincts of both component animals and instead of fighting, just flies away.

With that finished, the struggle turns internal. Madeleine tries to argue that they are better together than they were independently. Jennifer and Ellie disagree, and lobotomize Madeleine's part of the brain, taking over the body entirely.

Whereas the previous movies discussed have focused on men frankensteining the perfect female body for mating purposes, *Patchwork* twists the idea around. Yes, the idea of creating the perfect woman is still here, but this time around, it's a woman turning to frankensteining technology to perfect herself (with a man's help). It's more efficient. Why bother building a perfect mate, when you can build a perfect you to attract the perfect mate?

Patchwork misses the opportunity to seriously comment on beauty standards. Sure, Madeleine wants to be prettier, but the problem is less her going overboard to meet the pressures of societal beauty standards and more that she's a psychopathic murderer. Even when she has "fixed" herself and has this new body, she is still killing people.

On the other hand, the film does present some interesting ideas about the lens through which we view other women's relationships to their bodies and lives, and the judgments we make about whether they are happy with those bodies and lives.

Madeleine picks Ellie and Jennifer to kill not at random, but because she believes they are not whole or happy in their lives or selves. Of course, it's easy for us to see people who aren't striving to meet beauty standards or social standards and assume they are failing rather than assuming they are not partaking.

Yes, Jennifer does not have a lot of friends because of her focus on work, and her relationship is an extramarital affair with her boss. Madeleine not only perceives this as a failure, she also makes the assumption that Jennifer feels like a failure as well and will be grateful for a new life. However, a lot of women find career success fulfilling and are perfectly happy not being part of traditional relationships. Similarly, Ellie enjoys hanging out at the bar and hooking up with random guys. Who is anyone to say that this is not a fulfilling life?

The idea of these stereotyped moral failings that need to be corrected is a key point in the film, though not explored completely or satisfyingly, and we end up with a couple of women who are stereotypes and Madeleine, who is the most unique and complex of the lot due to her zest for slaughtering people, though that's not fully examined either. That's fine, because at the end of the day, watching this frankenbabe on a dude-killing spree is cool too.

There's more to what makes Patchwork Woman's killing spree so fulfilling though, not to mention Sheetar's and Frankenhooker's. With these killing sprees, these three frankenbabes are fulfilling the screaming promise their great-grandmother made at the conclusion of *The Bride of Frankenstein*, a promise she was not able to follow through on thanks to the monster's if-I-can't-have-her-nobody-will murder/suicide.

The tragedy of the Bride is that she is boxed in so absolutely, that her options are to accept the wife/mother role prescribed for her or be killed. But her progeny found their way out of that box, by being the ones who do the killing. And at the end of each of their films, they live, happily. And through them, the Bride lives as well.

THE ART HISTORY LESSON (WITH FANGS)

In a seedy Los Angeles strip club, a woman in a stark red dress appears on a stage drenched in green light. She wears an angular red wig to match her dress. Her face is painted white. She sits unsmiling on a strange chair shaped like a muscular, headless man.

As the music builds, she slides to the floor. On all fours, she does a slow cat dance. Her movements are bold and abrupt to match the song playing around her, which sounds like something space aliens would produce after reading descriptions of David Bowie. Wearing black opera gloves with long, fake nails glued to the fingertips, she runs her hands over her body.

Eventually, she takes her dress off, revealing a body painted in wild geometries. A bra of coiled silver wires tries and fails to hide her bare breasts as she continues to dance around the stage, her moves becoming increasingly sexual. She climbs back onto her man-shaped chair, gyrating on its lap, before once again falling onto her knees and burying her face in its crotch as the music ends.

The crowd of drunks, ne'er-do-wells, and three out-of-place frat boys are stunned into silence for a moment before breaking into applause and raining dollar bills onto the stage. This is Katrina, two-thousand-year-old queen of vampires, played by groundbreaking model/musician/actress Grace Jones in 1986's *Vamp*. Of the thousands of vampires that have appeared onscreen throughout film history, none has ever made an entrance like this.

As brilliant as this entrance is, there's more to it than meets the eye. The body painting is by Keith Haring, part of an ongoing collaboration with Jones. Haring was an artist and gay rights activist whose career began in the early 80s with unique graffiti he did around New York City's subway system. His exuberant art frequently depicts joyful beings and big hearts. After his graffiti work caught the public's attention, it also caught the art world's attention, and by the end of the 80s, his art was appearing in major museums and galleries.

Haring first painted Jones's body for *Interview Magazine*

in a now iconic photo session organized by Andy Warhol and photographed by Robert Mapplethorpe, two other renowned artists. When it came time to film *Vamp*, Jones brought in several of her artist friends and collaborators to help her bring her vision of Katrina to life, starting with Keith Haring. This would be the second, but not the last, of their body painting collaborations, and it makes the scene nothing less than museum-worthy.

Grace Jones had already established herself as a model and an adventurous musician, working first in disco and then moving into a version of new wave that melded reggae, funk, and other sounds that made it stand out from most of what played on MTV at the time. It's her song playing as she dances, one she wrote for the film and which has never been released elsewhere. She designed the choreography as well. The filmmakers had asked for a more traditionally sultry stripper dance, but Jones delivered her far more artsy dance instead. It's not something you expect to see at a strip club. To be fair though, you don't expect to see a vampire there either.

This dance is witnessed by three frat boys, or technically speaking, wannabe frat boys, who as an initiation to their frat have been tasked with hiring a stripper for a party. Not surprisingly, they are in awe, and Katrina is their immediate choice. AJ, the ringleader of the three, goes backstage to proposition her.

One of the most endearing parts of this movie is how it begins as a boner comedy, that omnipresent genre of the 80s in which a group of loser guys go on a mission to have a sexual adventure, before becoming a performance art film as soon as the guys set foot in the strip club. Even as their mission falls apart, they still goof and joke and sling one-liners as if in a totally different movie.

Not surprisingly, AJ's propositioning of Katrina goes badly. In her lair in the back room, she wordlessly seduces him. Just as he thinks his mission is a success, she vamps out. Her vampire form is truly monstrous, as horrific here as she was beautiful on stage, an animalistic, vicious ghoul who digs her teeth into AJ's throat, not just sucking his blood, but tearing it out, before lifting her head with a hiss-scream of celebration, one of the few sounds to come out of her mouth the whole film.

Here Jones becomes a canvas for an entirely different sort of art. 1922's *Nosferatu* was groundbreaking in the vampire film genre, featuring Max Schreck as a bald, pointy-eared, long-fingered ghoul who was truly menacing. But that vision of the vampire fell to the wayside after 1931's *Dracula*, which opted instead for the more handsome vampiric vision presented by Bela Lugosi. For many years, viewers could expect their vampires to be beautiful, their bloodsucking more like a sex act than a violent feeding.

With *Vamp* though, makeup artist Greg Cannom brought a return to the ideal of the vampire being physically scary. Katrina's vampire form is all harsh ridges and heavy shadows, an animal with piercing eyes and a mouth full of fangs that could never be described as elegant. Like Nosferatu, she has long fingers with which to tear her victims apart.

Cannom would continue to push his vision of a monstrous vampire, most notably in the next year's hit *The Lost Boys.* He also worked 1991's *Subspecies,* a vampire film from Full Moon Studios, the makers of the *Puppet Master* films (which we will discuss in another chapter), as well as the more mainstream productions *Bram Stoker's Dracula* in 1992 for which he won an Academy Award for best makeup and hair, and *Blade* in 1998. All of these films featured monstrous visions of vampiredom.

I have nothing against a sexy vampire, but if I want to watch a monster movie, I want to see a monster, and we can thank Cannom for making that more common in the vampire genre today.

After discovering Katrina and the rest of the strippers and staff are vampires, one of the remaining frat boys tries to warn the rest of the clubgoers. He shouts, "Call the police! These people, they're all vampires."

A crowd member replies, "That doesn't make them bad people!"

The remaining frat boys team up with the one non-vampire stripper to escape, only to learn the whole neighborhood is teeming with the undead. A chase ensues through a maze of purple- and green-lit LA back alleys filled with scaffolding, empty barrels, dumpsters, and billowing fog, before the boys and their new stripper friend climb into the sewer hoping to evade their pursuers. Instead, they end up in a coffin-filled lair, right as the vampires are shuffling back in for their dawn-fearing slumber. Thankfully, there are several barrels of gasoline sitting there for some reason, which our heroes conveniently tip over and use to light the vampires on fire.

The heroes are not out of danger yet. They still have Katrina to contend with. She finds them in the sewer and captures the good stripper, threatening to bite her. Luckily, they had earlier broken into a sporting goods store, where one of our frat boys scored a bow and arrow. He shoots Katrina in the mouth, right between her jagged fangs. She releases her captive, but Katrina is not dead yet. Well, not fully dead. She is a vampire, after all. She removes the arrow and continues her attack.

Katrina is in full-on Nosferatu mode now. She has ditched the wigs to show off her bald head and looks feral with fangs bared, reaching out with her long fingers. This is what a vampire is supposed to look like! The bow-toting frat boy lures her toward a patch of sunlight and she begins to melt. She falls to the ground. Her life force floats out of her in the form of a green cloud. Then her face blows up! Her skin shoots from the front of her skull, revealing her bony, fanged visage. Finally, the rest of her flesh melts off. With the last of her power, she lifts her skeletal hand and whips a boney bird to the heroes as they escape.

Grace Jones deserves a lot of credit for taking a role in what would have been an average, low-budget film and creating a one-of-a-kind vision of a vampire. The filmmakers gave her free reign to shape her character, and she brought in her artist friends to make the role something unique.

In an interview with the *Guardian*, she said, "I never

wanted to move to Hollywood—I never did—so when I first went there to film *Vamp*, I surrounded myself with friends: Keith Haring (who body-painted Jones), Andy Warhol, Antonio Lopez [both of whom worked on set design]. I lived like a vampire: up all night, asleep all day." She even, according to an interview with *The Today Show*, took up smoking to know what addiction might feel like, to understand how a vampire might feel toward blood.

She brought in her own makeup artists and costumes. Katrina is constantly changing looks, going from one bold, brightly-colored outfit to the next. Often, she wears elaborate headdresses with coiled and curved wires, which look like something out of the Museum of Modern Art. Items are pulled together from different time periods, different cultures. Katrina is a narcissist, Jones admits, but all the costume choices have another purpose. They "show all the different lives Katrina has been through."

And it works. Jones also made the bold decision to not speak throughout the movie. She does not have a single line. She doesn't need one. Through her fashion choices, her dances, her sets, her gestures, her expressions, she creates a story of a vampire with a history unlike any that came before or after.

THE WEREWOLF SISTERS

While werewolf women have a long history in cinema, going back to 1944's *Cry of the Werewolf* and up through the *Howling* films of the 80s, none are more iconic than the sisters Ginger and Brigitte of the *Ginger Snaps* trilogy. The *Ginger Snaps* films dispose of the lore and history that often bog down the genre, replacing them with a meaningful and brutal conversation about growing up as girls.

In his essay, "Monster Movies: A Sexual Theory,"

Professor Walter Evans states that monster movies reflect the transition from childhood to adulthood, a transition that young people "do not understand, cannot control, and have some reason to fear. Mysterious feelings and urges begin to develop and they find themselves strangely fascinated with disturbing new physical characteristics."

Ginger Snaps (2000) takes this subtext and moves it to text. The film is as much about puberty as it is about werewolves. The two run so closely parallel to each other in the narrative, they become inseparable.

"United against life as we know it," the two sisters—Ginger, 16, and Brigitte, 15—proclaim at the outset of the first movie. The suicide-obsessed teens spend their days in the basement filming scenes of their own death. They share the film in class, but it doesn't endear them to their teacher, nor to their classmates. In fact, it adds to their troubles. The sisters are the targets of relentless bullying that only pushes them closer to each other.

Meanwhile, their small town has been plagued by a series of gruesome attacks on local dogs, so frequent and intense that canine corpses seem to pop up everywhere throughout the first act. Characters are constantly stumbling onto, and often into, gory pet death scenes. I can't understate how intense this aspect of the film is. I watch a lot of horror movies, so it takes a lot to get to me, but the night of rewatching *Ginger Snaps,* I woke in a sweat from a dream in which I was forced to climb a mountain of dead dogs, my limbs sinking into their decaying meat. Shudder.

Despite knowing about the dog deaths, the girls go out one night on a revenge mission against one of their bullies. Their plan: to kidnap her dog and fake its death on video, which they would then share with their bully. Before they can do that, they stumble onto a real dead dog. Instead of being weirded out, these two out-goth everyone by being excited. Now they don't have to fake a dead dog. They can use this actual dog corpse as a stand-in for their bully's dog.

Before they can do any of this, a stream of blood drips down the inside of Ginger's leg. "I got the curse," she proclaims. Then she gets another curse—the dog's killer, a massive werewolf, attacks her, dragging her into the woods. She escapes and flees with Brigitte. In the process, the local drug dealer crashes into and kills the werewolf. It's a convenient plot device, but also one of the things that makes *Ginger Snaps* so effective. The film does not fall into the trap of getting bogged down with finding out who the werewolf was, hunting it down, and killing it. The film can focus on the main theme: becoming a werewolf. And also going through puberty.

Ginger recovers quickly from her bites. From there, she begins growing fur and a little wiggly tail that she desperately straps to her leg with electrical tape. Even worse, she starts to like boys. Gasp! She grows more distant from her sister as she tries to navigate the changes that come from both adolescence and wolfing out. To be sure, the connection between adolescence and werewolfery did not come into this film by accident. This is not me trying to shoehorn meaning into a film where none exists. In an interview with *Fangoria*, *Ginger Snaps* writer Karen Walton explains that she worked hard to "weave up the metaphor and really 'go there,' layer the social/gender stuff in, emotionally."

She continues by saying, "My uterus and I were just trying to write something my girlfriends and I would actually want to go see, something that felt true to being a young woman at that age—to us." And it does feel true, which should come as no surprise. It's worth pointing out that the *Ginger Snaps* trilogy is the only monster movie franchise with every entry written or co-written by a woman.

Ginger, after some experimenting, and some unprotected sex, and killing the neighbor's dog, makes an awful discovery about her new self. "I get this ache. I thought it was for sex, but it's to tear everything to fucking pieces." This is one of the most frightening moments in the film, the moment when she discovers she is no longer who she believed herself to be, and there is no going back.

As Ginger's reign of terror begins, Brigitte teams up with the drug dealer who accidentally killed the original werewolf. Turns out he knows a thing or two about lycanthropy and how to stop it. Together, they eventually come up with a solution: the curse can be healed with an injection of a serum created from the flowers of the Monkshood plant, also known as *wolfsbane.* The drug dealer guy is stocked up on needles and syringes, and the preparation is a lot like that of heroin.

In the finale, all of Ginger's confusion is gone. She has accepted her adult, werewolf self. She remorselessly kills the teacher who didn't like her and her sister's suicide film, along with a janitor. "I'm a goddamn force of nature," she declares.

While accepting that you're a killing machine isn't great, obviously, the idea that she has accepted herself during this intense time of transition is powerful, and is what makes her character resonate so strongly with audiences. I know I'm not alone in that, even as a fully grown woman mostly settled into my adult life, I have days when I look in the mirror and I'm not sure who I am or what I'm doing. Maybe I need to stare into my eyes and declare, "I'm a goddamn force of nature." Maybe we all should.

During the final confrontation, Ginger and Brigitte argue about the new distance between them. Ginger, of course, likes who she is now. She wants her sister to grow up with her. Knowing she has a way to heal lycanthropy, Brigitte concedes to her sister's plan in order to buy some time. She cuts open her hand and exposes herself to her sister's blood, initiating the process of becoming a werewolf herself.

Ultimately, Brigitte fails to heal her sister's lycanthropy, and it's doubtful that is what her sister wants anyway. In their confrontation, though, Ginger, in her fully complete wolf form now, is accidentally killed. The film ends with Brigitte crying over her sister's body.

One of the most interesting aspects of the film is how

the transformation to a werewolf is not a sudden thing that occurs with the full moon. It is a gradual and permanent process that takes place over a month, beginning with a bit of fur and a nub of a tail and culminating with Ginger turning into a giant, mostly hairless wolf. While this forfeits the shock value of the sudden transformation seen in the traditional werewolf movie, it allows us to, in a sense, go through the change with her. We get to see her trying to shave off the excess hair. We get to see the tail-tucking struggles. We get to see how cool Ginger looks in her penultimate wolf form, still mostly human, but with white hair, wolflike eyes and brow, and claws.

We get to see special effects artist Paul Jones's brilliant design of her final form, when she's fully wolfed out. It's a unique design that keeps with films like *American Werewolf in London*, but is furless, other than a few shocks of remaining white hair. The film used all practical effects at a time when the industry was switching over to CGI, and the slow transformation over the course of the film gives the audience the opportunity to savor this last gasp of a craft that has become increasingly rare.

In Evans's essay, he explains that the more traditional vision of the werewolf's "bloody attacks—which occur regularly every month—are certainly related to the menstrual cycle which suddenly and mysteriously commands the body of every adolescent girl." On the surface, *Ginger Snaps* would seem to subvert this idea with its less cyclical approach to the werewolf myth. That isn't the story being told here though. *Ginger Snaps* is more interested in how first menstruation marks the transition into adulthood, which, as sudden as it may seem at the time, is indeed a gradual and permanent change.

The preeminent film of menstruation and monstrosity is 1976's *Carrie*, the Brian DePalma adaptation of the Stephen King novel. I'm going to get a lot of flack for this, but *Ginger Snaps* does it better. In *Carrie*, the title character's telekinetic powers are invoked by her first period, like how Ginger's werewolf transformation begins at the same time. But where *Ginger Snaps* plunges into the awkwardness of a changing body and changing interests, *Carrie* seems content to focus on bullies. Bullies are an important aspect in *Ginger Snaps*, but the bullying/bullied relationship is also far more nuanced, especially in how one of the sisters' male bullies becomes the target of Ginger's newfound sexual appetite, before returning to bully status. While *Carrie* deserves its place as a classic, it fails in fully portraying the horrors of adolescence in a real way. That's exactly where *Ginger Snaps* succeeds.

Interestingly, Katherine Isabelle, who plays Ginger, also starred in the 2002 remake of *Carrie*, this time switching sides and playing one of the title character's main bullies. Beginning her acting career before she was even 10 years old, Isabelle has appeared in more than 100 films and TV shows. Many of her roles have been in the horror genre, including an appearance in the *Goosebumps* TV show of the late 90s and the lead in the 2012 feminist cult classic *American Mary*. "I didn't set out to do horror films," she says in an interview with *Red Carpet News*. "It's just, the best characters and some of the best stories I've come across happen to have been in horror."

Emily Perkins, who plays Brigitte, also started her acting career as a child. Her filmography is slightly less horror-centric than her co-star's, though one of her early roles was in the 1990 adaptation of Stephen King's *It.* Incidentally, both actresses appeared in episodes of *X-Files* in the late 90s as well, hinting they were on a similar career trajectory.

Two wildly different sequels to *Ginger Snaps* were produced back-to-back and both released in 2004. It makes perfect sense that the follow-ups to a film that so daringly discards genre formulas have no interest in rehashing the story of their predecessor. In one sense, that is a major strength because when you watch the sequels, you never get the feeling you've seen the story before. In another sense, though, this means leaving behind the theme of adolescence in favor of creating more straightforward horror films. Though certainly not too straightforward, especially in the case of the second sequel.

First though, let's look at *Ginger Snaps 2: Unleashed.* The film opens with Brigitte alone, injecting the purple monkshood serum to ward off her change into a werewolf. Monkshood isn't a cure after all, as the characters believe in the first film. It only slows down the transformation. So she roams from town to town, staying in hotel rooms and shooting up, on the run from a mysterious male werewolf. The male doesn't want to kill her. He wants to mate with her. (Gross. If there's one thing worse than a stalker, it is a stalker who is also a werewolf.)

Her stalker finds her and attacks her. She escapes but passes out somewhere. She's found and brought to a weird rehab facility on the assumption she's a drug addict. The place is a mess. It's dark, rundown, and dingy. One wing is closed and falling apart, complete with holes in the wall.

This doesn't seem to be voluntary rehab either. Brigitte is not free to go. Perhaps Canada's healthcare system is more serious about helping people overcome addiction. Here in the U.S., I know people who are on waitlists or who have driven long distances to find space in a rehab facility. Meanwhile, this place is picking people up off the street, not even checking if they are doing real drugs or injecting anti-werewolf serum? Unbelievable.

Not that it's a wonderful place. In addition to the aforementioned state of disrepair, there's also a creepy nurse who trades all the women residents drugs for sex. Oh yeah, and a little girl who is not who she seems to be.

"If you keep me here, people are going to die," Brigitte warns the administrator. The administrator mistakes that for a threat and locks Brigitte in her room.

The movie suffers from the lack of Ginger. She appears occasionally as a ghost, but not frequently enough to maintain the sister dynamic that helped make the first film so great. There's not much about adolescence and growing up, other than a scene where Brigitte is masturbating and then looks at her palm to find it covered with hair, a clever reference to the old wives' tale. That said, the twist ending is unique and helps propel *Unleashed* far above the typical sequel.

Still, it feels like a basic horror film when sandwiched between the original and *Ginger Snaps Back: The Beginning.* The final film in the trilogy isn't really a sequel. It's not really a prequel either, despite it frequently being referred to as such. This film reunites Brigitte and Ginger and reimagines their story in the Canadian wilderness in 1815. Lost in the woods, the sisters make their way to Fort Bailey, a trading fort, which they quickly learn is besieged by werewolves who haunt the surrounding area.

Again, no metaphor here about growing up. Instead, the film hones in on the relationship between the sisters as they try to figure out what to do while the men of the fort argue and fuss. Like in the original, Ginger is bitten, this time by a werewolf child kept locked up by his father, who runs the fort. The drama is done well and feels akin to John Carpenter's *The Thing*, carrying some of the same paranoia elements, as the fort's men worry about who among them may have been bitten, but adding the attackers from without and the twist of the introduction of two women, who have no interest in the men's drama and stick together, further strengthening their bond.

As expected in such a film, the men self-destruct. By this time, Ginger is far into her transformation. The men cast her out of the fort, but she returns as everything is falling apart. In a just world, the image of Ginger, in her black cloak, hood pulled up, face enshadowed except for her bloody lips, opening the fort gates to tread over the snow-covered ground as her wolfpack floods in around her, would be considered among the most iconic in horror. It's such a powerful scene that it makes you want to run out into the woods and get bitten yourself. (Please don't do this. The odds of getting bitten by a werewolf and not a regular old wolf are very slim. Stay safe.)

The werewolf action that follows is the best in the trilogy, and truly among the best in all of werewolf filmdom. I know this sounds like hyperbole, but it's true. Robert Kurtzman, Howard Berger, and their KNB EFX team have created some of the most memorable special effects in horror history, and their work here stands out. The werewolves are vicious, gruesome, and totally believable as they systematically maul the men at the fort.

And the sisters walk away from all the destruction. They walk into the woods. Unlike in the first movie, where the sisters' pact is broken in the ending with Brigitte cradling her dead sister, here it is Ginger who holds Brigitte, but there's no tragedy to be seen. They repeat their pact and hold each other's bleeding hands, saying, "Together forever."

While *Unleashed* seems weak in comparison to the other films in the trilogy, it's still safe to call this one of the most perfect horror franchises ever created. Each film is distinct, holds its own, and is a joy to watch. Part of me wishes the series had continued, but a practical effects–driven, femme-centric werewolf trilogy released during the dying days of video rental stores? The fact that the franchise even made it to three films is a big deal, and we should cherish them.

THE LIVING DEAD GIRL

The zombie genre is built on the fear of a nameless, faceless horde of reanimated corpses. The fear isn't only about being consumed by the horde, but also of losing one's individuality and becoming part of the horde. Over the years though, a small number of zombies have risen out of the mass of mindless brain-eaters to stand on their own, to hold onto their individuality or create a new individuality, at least for a few precious moments: Bub from *Day of the Dead* (1978), the baby zombie from *Dead Alive* (1992), and Fido from

Fido (2006). But only one stands out as the coolest, most badass zombie of all time: Julie from 1993's *Return of the Living Dead 3*. With her dyed red hair, torn fishnets, and freshly-dead skin pierced with all manner of scrap metal, she cuts an imposing figure, an undead S&M queen like no other.

The third film in the *Return of the Living Dead* franchise, this sequel bears no meaningful connection to the previous films outside of the theme of zombies created by toxic chemicals. On the surface, it presents itself as a tragic tale of doomed love like Romeo and Juliet, but the zombie element adds a layer to the tragedy that perhaps the filmmakers had not intended.

The movie opens with Julie, still living, and her boyfriend, Curt, sneaking onto the military base where Curt's dad works. They witness Curt's dad and other members of the military experimenting on a corpse, using the reanimating chemical trioxin to bring the corpse back to life, then shoot it with a special bullet that is supposed to put it into a state of frozen suspension. The bullet doesn't work though, and the corpse goes on a rampage. Julie and Curt ditch the scene.

Back at Curt's house, Julie and Curt have sex. They are interrupted when Curt's dad returns home to inform Curt he's being transferred to another state. An argument breaks out and Curt's dad says some mean things about Julie, thinking she's beneath his son. The two lovers run away on Curt's motorcycle with plans to flee the state. The plan goes awry when they crash and Julie is killed.

In W. W. Jacobs's classic short story "The Monkey's Paw," the new owners of the wish-granting paw are clearly warned that the wishes come with a price, and when they ignore the warning and use a wish to bring back their dead son, they know he is not going to return the way he was. So, too, does Curt know, from having already witnessed what happens when trioxin is used to reanimate the dead, that Julie will not be the same person she was before. But, like the parents in "The Monkey's Paw," Curt's desire to have his love returned to him pushes him to seek out the trioxin to grant his wish anyway. He sneaks Julie's corpse back onto the base and reanimates her.

"My heart," Julie says upon awakening. "I can't feel my heart." The line is portentous. What love she and Curt shared prior to death is no longer there. Curt is blind to this though. He still envisions a life together, insisting everything will be okay despite Julie's continued pleading about her hunger.

Curt takes Julie to a convenience store. She goes wild on the Hostess snacks endcap, but they don't do her any good. She lets each bite tumble out of her mouth in disgust. But when some criminals attempt to rob the store, she snatches one of their arms on the way out, taking a big bite. She now knows what she is hungry for. In the holdup, the owner of the store is shot. Julie and Curt try to take him to the hospital, but all Julie can think of is food.

Julie finds a piece of metal, a rusty spring, in the van. To assuage her hunger, she uses it to cut herself. "The pain helps. The pain makes the hunger go away," she says.

But not permanently. The trip to the hospital is cut short, because Julie eats the injured store owner's brains.

She and Curt get into an argument. He's disgusted by her. She tells him it's his fault. He brought her back. "You should have left me dead." She runs off and finds her way onto one of LA's oldest bridges, the 7th Street Bridge, looking down on the LA River. Curt tries to stop her, but she jumps off and somehow disappears in the not even ankle-deep water below.

Curt goes in search of her, but first encounters a homeless man who calls himself the Riverman. As they walk through the river barely getting their shoes wet, the Riverman exclaims that the darkness swallowed her up. He tries to stop Curt from searching, saying the woman clearly does not want to be found.

With the Riverman behind him, Curt eventually finds Julie in a tangle of garbage. At that moment, the criminals from the earlier store robbery appear. They want revenge on Julie for the bite that has made one of them sick. The Riverman leads Curt and Julie into a tunnel, and the three of them take refuge in a pump room the Riverman has made his home.

The Riverman takes watch outside, giving the couple what passes for a tender moment. Only it becomes clear how superficial their love is. Julie, obviously struggling, is forced to listen as Curt tells her about the life they will have together, how he's going to get a gig in a band, and how she can even come and watch him play! When she asks, "Why are you doing this to me?" It barely even registers to him. He's concocted a version of love, but she's more the target of it than an active participant. Perhaps she never was—did he ever really see her? As it stands now, he has resurrected her, without her consent, and has given no effort to finding out what she wants. She is more of an object to him than anything else, which is fitting considering the history of the zombie in and outside of film.

In their essay, "A Zombie Manifesto," zombie scholars Sarah Juliet Lauro and Karen Embry state, "In its history, and in its metaphors, the zombie is most often a slave." In folklore, zombies were created to provide labor. In films like George Romero's *Dawn of the Dead*, they represent slavery to capitalism and consumerism. Here, Julie has been recreated by Curt to fulfill the role of a domestic slave, a partner who has no ambitions of her own and will happily want nothing more than to watch him play in a band, even though he admits to the Riverman he hasn't actually learned any instruments. When Julie exerts her own needs, Curt is disgusted. Granted, her needs are primarily to eat brains, but still. Needs are needs.

The criminals find the couple's hiding spot. Curt steps outside to join the Riverman and attempt to deal with them. Finally, Julie has a moment alone. Fighting her hunger, she cuts herself apart. She finds every piece of scrap metal she can. She pierces her lips. She jabs needle-like scraps through her fingertips, forming makeshift claws. She jabs shards into her forehead and cheeks. Her most utilitarian modification is a length of rope threaded through her palm, the other end tied to a rock she can use to bash open skulls to get to the tasty brains.

She's not only using the pain to distract her from hunger. She's asserting her individuality. She claims, "I'm losing myself, Curt," but the line shouldn't be misread as meaning this modified version of her is her lost self. This is her self reclaimed.

At the outset of the movie, there's a fleeting scene of her holding her hand over her lighter, feeling her palm burning from the heat. Her friends try to stop her, and they joke about it, but this is her. She likes her body like this. This isn't new to the dead version of her. This is an extension of the her she was holding back in life.

It's also a perfect extension of actress Melinda Clarke's career at the time. When she auditioned for the role of Julie, she had recently finished doing a play called *Vicious*, about tragicouple Sid and Nancy. She, of course, played Nancy Spungen. She moved seamlessly from playing a heroin addict to a brain addict, bringing the same punk-rock energy to the screen. Her makeup, with all the wild piercings and punctures, helped too, and in the commentary track on the blu-ray, she explains that she let all her scrap metal guide her movements, letting them lead her body.

Julie's zombie makeup has a punk-rock history too. In the same commentary, special effects production supervisor Thomas Rainone describes how he and director Brian Yuzna went to the first Lollapalooza festival and ended up catching a performance by Mr. Lifto of the Jim Rose Circus. Lifto's act involved lifting heavy objects from a variety of piercings. They suddenly realized what they wanted their zombie to look like.

Return of the Living Dead 3 was Clarke's first starring role. She went on to become famous for her parts in TV series like *The OC*, *CSI*, and *Nikita.* So far, *Return* is her only horror role, though she has dabbled in some horror-adjacent movies like *Spawn* and *Killer Tongue. Killer Tongue* was one of the weirdest films of the 90s. Clarke plays a woman whose body is taken over by a parasitic alien tongue who turns her into a sort of superhero, and also turns her poodles into drag queen sidekicks for some reason.

When Julie steps out in her newly-pierced form and kills the criminals who have been hunting her down, suddenly Curt is no longer interested. His dad appears with his special gun to subdue her, and he steps aside and lets him without any argument. Clearly this version of Julie is too much for him, and not the docile simpering object he had hoped to own when reanimating her.

Later, Curt ends up back at the military base with his dad. He wanders off among the cages filled with zombies. Eventually, he finds Julie, locked up. All the scrap metal has been removed. She's nearly naked, crouched, and simpering in the corner of the cage. Now he wants her back, now that she's reduced to a possessed object again. He breaks her out.

As the base falls into chaos and more zombie experiments go haywire, Curt is bitten. Now he too is destined to become a zombie. He leads Julie to the incinerator. Holding hands, they climb in together.

Though I wish Julie had a better ending, where she was allowed to be her badass scrapheap zombie self, I still love this movie. It has some of the sloppiest, gooiest, most creative zombie effects ever seen on film before or since. Five different special effects companies were brought in to work on it, the most ever on a single film, according to Rainone. The zombies were inspired by everything from industrial music to old EC comics and Alice Cooper tour posters.

More importantly, *Return of the Living Dead 3* paved the way for more unique takes on the zombie genre, where these films could be more than simple stories of the living versus hordes of the dead. Or they could be less than that—quieter stories of how lives and relationships can change in a world where the dead can return.

THE GIRL IN THE WELL

Lurking behind a curtain of wet black hair, her face never to be seen, is Sadako Yamamura. Sadako is the ghost of a young girl whose psychic powers were so strong when she was alive, she could kill a person with a mere thought. Now that she is dead, buried at the bottom of a hidden well, her powers are amplified. She haunts a videocassette, coming to kill anyone who watches it. There is only one way the watcher can avoid death, but it comes at a high cost. Released in 1998, *Ringu* has had an enormous impact on cinema, not just in Japan, but internationally. Its history goes back much further though.

The film begins with journalist Reiko Asakawa investigating the sudden, suspicious death of her niece. She hears rumors of a mysterious videocassette that was watched by her niece and three other high school students, all of whom died exactly one week after watching.

Asakawa tracks the VHS to a cabin where the four students snuck away for a night. She watches the video and is cursed. She summons her ex-husband, Ryuji, to help her break the curse. He watches the video too, so he is cursed as well. Then their child accidentally watches the VHS, giving them even more motivation to figure out how to break the curse.

Together, Asakawa and her ex learn about a psychic woman who jumped into a volcano after predicting its eruption, and her daughter, Sadako, who turns out to be an even more powerful psychic than her mother. How do they learn this? Conveniently, Ryuji is also psychic, so he mostly gets the backstory from visions while visiting Sadako's extended family.

At the last minute, they guess that Sadako must be near the cabin. They return there to find an old covered well below the cabin, which was built over it. Upon touching the well, Ryuji psychically sees that Sadako was killed and dumped inside. Together Asakawa and Ryuji excavate Sadako's bones and report her murder to the police. Asakawa's week elapses and she stays alive. She and Ryuji part ways, assuming they have broken the curse. But then Sadako comes for Ryuji, crawling out of his TV and stopping his heart when his week is up.

Asakawa realizes she did one thing differently than Ryuji. She copied the tape and passed it on to someone else to watch. When she passed the tape onto Ryuji, she broke her own curse. She realizes there is only one way to break the curse on her child, so she phones her grandparents. The movie ends as she drives toward their house and dark clouds gather above.

Sadako is unique among monsters in that she isn't particularly monstrous, yet is absolutely terrifying. It's all in her movements as she crawls out of the well. At a time when practical effects had reached a peak and CGI had yet to take off, the filmmakers resorted to one of the simplest cinematic tricks to create the twitchy, disjointed movements of their ghost: they simply filmed her going backward and reversed it. That's it, but even now, the result is extremely effective, the way Sadako's long black hair pours over the side of the well and onto the ground, as if dragging her body behind it, making it seem as if her hair has a life of its own, which later films in the series would exploit further.

Ring, the novel by Koji Suzuki upon which the film was based, was originally released in 1991, at the height of VHS's popularity. To say that the 1998 film is an adaptation of the novel is only partially true. Sadako is not a ghost in the novel. She does not come out of the well to snatch those she's cursed. She does not writhe out of the TV screen in the darkness to end their lives. There is no Sadako with the curtain of wet black hair hiding her face. Moreover, it is not truly her who is haunting the videocassette, and that's where the novel, which is more of a mystery with supernatural elements, gets complicated.

Before I explain who is haunting the videotape, I need to explain how the videotape became haunted. In the book, as in the film adaptation, Sadako is a powerful psychic. She is also extremely beautiful, and lusted after by men, who, of course, she rejects. Something important that is washed away in the film is that Sadako is intersex.

Musing on the idea of people with both male and female sex organs, Ryuji asks rhetorically, "Don't you think that's the ultimate symbol of power and beauty?" This is before he and Asakawa discover that Sadako is intersex. The subtext is that, even though the men who lust after Sadako do not know this about her, this is why they lust after her, why they find her irresistible.

In the novel, it is also why she dies. In the novel, she is not just killed and dumped into a well. She is raped by the doctor who is supposed to care for her while she is staying at a healthcare retreat. Upon seeing her genitals, he kills her and tosses her into a well.

The doctor admits all this to Asakawa and Ryuji in the book, and he goes further to say Sadako knew she was going to die. While she is not able to kill people with her mind in the book, her psychic powers are strong enough that she knows what is going to happen in the future. She knew it was her destiny to die this way.

After her death, she projects images that are eventually

picked up on an unused television channel in the cabin in the woods, where they are accidentally videotaped by someone who set the VCR to record the wrong channel. The images are projected by Sadako, but they are not Sadako, they are Sadako's child, the child not only of rape, but of rape by a man who was the last known carrier of a rare virus. This viral being of psychic rage creates a mechanism to do what all successful viruses must do to survive: spread. Only this virus spreads by VHS.

It's an epic concept, but the filmmakers were right to make Sadako into a vengeful ghost and put her front and center. Though it did not come from the novel, the idea of Sadako the vengeful ghost did not originate with the 1998 film either. Her origins go back much, much further. She's firmly rooted in Japan's historic ghost story tradition, rebuilt for the video age.

Director Hideo Nakata is clearly a fan of ghosts. His two previous films had ghostly elements. In particular, *Don't Look Up* (1996) features a woman ghost born of a piece of old, undeveloped film. While that movie was not a success, it's easy to see how the concept would pave the way for his adaptation of *Ring*.

Then there is the well. While the well has no explicit supernatural power in the novel, Nakata drew a connection to it from an old Japanese ghost story. In an interview with *Offscreen*, Nakata explains, "There's actually a story with a well, called 'Bancho Sarayasaiki,' which relates to this story in the sense that maybe the well is haunted by evil spirits. I myself when I lived in the countryside in Japan saw a well, about 5 meters deep, which is maybe not that deep, but for me as a child, it seemed like a bottomless hell."

Going back to at least the mid-1700s, "Bancho Sarayasaiki" is the story of Okiku, a servant girl lusted after by one of her master's men. She spurns his advances again and again. He kills her and throws her into a well. She comes back as a vengeful ghost. Sound familiar?

But "Bancho Sarayasaiki" wasn't the sole, or even the biggest, inspiration Nakata pulled from when creating his film version of Sadako. In the same interview he also mentions *The Ghost of Yotsuya*, a 1959 film based on a much older kabuki play, again about a scorned woman who comes back as a vengeful ghost, clad in a white kimono with long black hair. "I might say that I have studied all these," he says, "and the ancient histories and traditions of Japan." In fact, these vengeful women *yurei*, the Japanese word for ghosts, are so plentiful they have their own ghost subset: Onryo.

Nakata mentions, in an interview with *Ain't It Cool News*, that Sadako's hair was an intentional move. "[To] Japanese people, Asian people, long black hair of a woman has somehow a kind of supernatural power or emotion just by itself, so if you look at *Kwaidan* [a 1964 movie from Japan that also features a female ghost with long black hair] there is a kind of subconscious fear for women's long black hair by itself."

So Nakata took what was already a popular novel, tied it into Japan's long-standing tradition of ghost stories, and created what has become the most successful and expansive Japanese horror franchise of all time.

The Ring franchise is my favorite type of franchise. It's a convoluted mess of book-to-film adaptations, remakes, sequels, manga, international remakes, more sequels, more manga, audio dramas, and on and on, with Sadako at the heart of it all. She is the calm at the center of this storm of evolving content that swirls around her, standing there, watching through her curtain of hair.

The 1998 adaptation of the film was not actually the first. A 1995 made-for-television version stuck a bit closer to the book's plot, but was not a success. Despite this spotty history, when it came time to make the 1998 version, the producers were so confident it would do well that they made the sequel simultaneously.

While they were right about *Ringu* being a success, they were wrong about the sequel, *Spiral. Spiral* (1998) is based on the book sequel of the same name, and as such goes more in depth on the idea of the video as virus. Unfortunately, audiences weren't interested and the film failed. That did not stop the producers though. They were committed to starting a franchise, so they simply pretended *Spiral* didn't exist and made a second part two.

Ring 2 (1999) follows more closely the events of the 1998 film, with some interesting changes. Sadako isn't bound strictly to the rules of the curse anymore. It's not just her videotape that can curse you. Merely learning about her story is enough, so Asakawa's journal where she documented what she learned about Sadako in the 1998 film becomes as powerful as the video.

Evolution is critical to the success of this franchise, necessary even. Although the book was released during the VHS boom, the 1998 film came at the tail end, when the format was already fading in favor of DVD. There was no way Sadako could remain a ghost haunting a VHS, and watching how different creators push her into new territory and how it changes with the tellings is not only part of the fun, but appropriate for a story about urban legends.

The first international remake of *The Ring* was 1999's *Ring Virus*, from South Korea. Interestingly, this film went back to the original novel as the primary source material. This is the only iteration of the franchise to be true to Sadako as being intersex, and not only emphasizes that this is a key source of her strength, but that people like her were historically worshiped as gods. It also more explicitly states that her being intersex is the reason for her death, that her rapist killed her after realizing this. The film turns the queer dial up a notch, and it's sad that no other adaptation has been willing to delve into this aspect of who Sadako is and was intended to be.

In 2002, the American remake was released. This was the first Japanese horror movie ever to be remade by Hollywood, setting off a boom that would continue with *The Grudge* and many others. The American version renames Sadako as Samara and strips her of some of her power, choosing to show her face. It replaces all the subtleties of the original with over-the-top nonsense, like a whole subplot about horse deaths that begins with a horse jumping off a ferry into the propeller blades. The cursed video itself is heavy-handed, with images of giant centipedes and a box full of severed fingers for some reason. Then there's the obnoxious subliminal ring images that flash between scenes.

Back in Japan, 2000's *Ring 0: Birthday* was where the franchise started to go off the rails in the best way possible. Like the best horror movie monsters, Sadako only appears onscreen for a matter of minutes in the original. In this prequel though, she's the star of the show, turned into a Carrie-like telekinetic wannabe theater star who is misunderstood and mistreated by her colleagues.

Ring 0: Birthday was the last film in the franchise to fully feature a human actor portraying Sadako, with Yukie Nakama, a former singer and bit-part actress stepping into the role for the first and only time.

Over the years, there have been nearly as many actresses playing Sadako as there have been *Ring* films. The most well-known is Rie Inō, who portrayed Sadako in the 1998 film. Inō was already a veteran of kabuki theater when she was cast as Sadako, having begun her career when she was about 10 years old. She was over 30 when she was cast in *Ring*. Over time, Sadako would be portrayed as younger and younger, but that was not the case in the novel, or in the 1998 film. In both, Sadako was an adult at the time of her death. Oddly, Inō was not cast as Sadako in the initial sequel to the 1998 film, *Spiral*, but the producers brought her back for *Ring 2* when *Spiral* failed. Perhaps they recognized that she was a key part of the formula that made the 1998 film such a success.

Unfortunately, that was the last time Inō played Sadako. The role has been somewhat of a revolving door. One of the biggest stars to play the role was Bae Doona, who starred in the Korean adaptation. It was her first role, but she went on to international success in films like *Sympathy for Mr. Vengeance*, *Cloud Atlas*, and *Rebel Moon.* She might be most recognized by horror fans as the star of the medieval zombie series, *Kingdom.*

Sadly, in recent films, Sadako has been digitally animated and not portrayed by an actor.

Starting with *Sadako 3D*, the franchise ditches human actors as the ghost, not to mention the *Ring* title, along with the lore developed in the previous movies. Gone is the VHS tape, in favor of internet video clips. Watching the video clip no longer makes the viewer's heart stop. That's not shocking enough for 3D. Instead, viewers violently kill themselves. Sadako has become a history-less ghoul, taking full advantage of the 3D gimmick to lunge and jump out of the screen. Her hair has become longer and prehensile, moving wildly. Her goal has changed too. Now, she wants to find a living body to possess, but the body must belong to someone who is psychic.

The first of the two 3D movies, released in 2012, serves as a soft reboot to the series, and it is pure, beautiful monster nonsense. A weird artist guy is trying to summon Sadako, so he kidnaps a bunch of women who look like her, dresses them up like her, and throws them into her well. He hopes these sacrifices will appease Sadako and make her reappear.

She doesn't, so he tries something else. He makes a new cursed video and uploads it online. That seems to work, and the video spreads, causing a rash of suicides. A schoolteacher of one of the video's victims takes it upon herself to investigate, ultimately watching the video herself. She's not a regular victim though. She's psychic and the intended new body for Sadako.

The finale features all the women who the weird artist guy dumped into the well becoming Sadako demons. Their legs twist and distort, forcing them to crawl. They crawl up out of the well and go on a rampage. Moving like crickets, they hunt the schoolteacher. The series has now become a pure monster movie. No subtext. No nuance. Just ghouls doing what ghouls do best.

An interesting promotion began with the release of *Sadako 3D*. The film studio reached out to find the perfect collaborator on merchandise. Who better to team up with one of the scariest ghosts in cinema history than . . . Hello Kitty?!?! It might not make sense, but it worked. Hello Kitty and Sadako were mashed together to create a Hello Kitty with long black hair over her face, complete with pink barrettes to hold it in place as she pawed her way out of her well. This mashup was popular enough that it continued with a new barrage of Hello Kitty x Sadako merch with the release of each subsequent Sadako film, beginning a cute-ification of the titular ghost that would bleed back into the series.

2019's *Sadako* ditched the 3D and featured the return of

director Hideo Nakata. In this version, a deranged mother summons Sadako to possess her psychic daughter, who she has been keeping in a closet. As expected, things don't go according to plan. Mom ends up dying by Sadako's suicide curse, while the daughter escapes into the world.

Even though the movie is a bit more serious in tone and truer to the 1998 version than the 3D films, it was accompanied by a pair of adorable manga that are my favorite visions of Sadako. The first, *Sadako-San and Sadako-Chan,* takes the film's initial concept as its launching point. Sadako comes to find the nameless girl who has been locked in the closet. No possession takes place. Instead Sadako and the girl, nicknamed Sadako-Chan, which roughly translates to Little Sadako, decide to become content creators. Sadako never gets around to cursing anyone, on account of nobody having a TV anymore. On top of that, cursing people is a lot of work. On the plus side, their videos start getting a lot of views, and monetizing them with ads seems more fun than cursing people. It builds on the previously established Hello Kitty–collab cuteness to create a story that nevertheless stays true to the 1998 film.

The second manga, *Sadako at the End of the World,* manages to be cute while hanging onto some of the bleakness of the early films. Here, Sadako is summoned by a couple of moppets who are surviving on their own following the apocalypse. They find and fix an old VCR and play Sadako's cursed tape. Sadako is a bit disappointed to learn the two girls might be the only surviving humans, because that would mean her cursing days are over. She encourages the girls to go off on a mission to find more people for Sadako to curse. Sadako doesn't mention the whole cursing part though. The girls just think they are going on an adventure. Interestingly, on the adventure, they meet Okiko, the aforementioned well-ghost of Japanese lore.

Sadako DX (2022) completely leaves all semblance of Sadako's backstory behind and takes a turn toward lighthearted comedy, finally bringing the tone established in the recent manga and cute toys into the realm of the cinematic. A fake mystic spreads the cursed video, thinking it wasn't real but wanting to generate fear and make money breaking the curse (and talking about it on talk shows). Alas, it is real. This time around, instead of showing abstract images, the video shows Sadako's point of view as she crawls out of the well and appears in front of the home of whoever is watching it. After that, the watcher has only 24 hours to break the curse.

Ayaka Ichijo is a 200-IQ high school student who does a weird thing that involves pressing her thumbs into her neck and flapping her hands to help her think. She's brought onto a talk show to debate the fake mystic, insisting curses aren't real. The mystic gives her the video, and admits his whole thing is an act. Ayaka's sister watches the video though, and it turns out the curse is real. Ayaka teams up with the influencer boyfriend of a girl who died from the curse, as well as a shut-in who refuses to leave his mom's basement and only communicates via video chat using a cat-face avatar. Together, this ragtag team must figure out how to break the curse.

After 24 hours, Sadako appears to the cursed individual, but not in her usual form, not at first. She appears as someone the cursed individual loves, often a deceased family member, like Ayaka's dad, before that person's hair sprouts out and morphs into Sadako to strangle the cursed individual with her long, black, prehensile locks.

The members of the group discover that Sadako does not want the curse to spread. What she really wants is to be watched, over and over, like a daily medication. To break the curse, all the viewer needs to do is watch the video again, a daily dose of Sadako, and all is reset for the day.

It's a fitting update to the series, which started out as a reinvention of Japanese ghost stories for a modern age, only to be reinvented again and again. Whatever name she goes by, all she wants is to be seen, known, and not forgotten. The girl from the well will live forever.

THE NAZI KILLER

Leeches are fascinating animals. They are also among the most hated animals on Earth, along with fellow bloodsuckers like ticks and mosquitos. In reality, of the 680 described species of leeches, only the smallest percentage suck blood, those in the subclass Hirudinida.

Leeches have existed since the middle Permian Period (273–259 million years ago). As a reminder, *Homo sapiens* have only been around a few hundred thousand years. According to Leech scientist Mark Siddal in an article from the *New York Times*, "the earliest land vertebrates may have been the first hosts for leeches." In other words, they've been sucking blood since before dinosaur times. Heck, they probably even sucked dinosaur blood. Can Dracula top that?

Is knowing how long they have existed enough to make you change your mind about these animals? No? What if I tell you about how leeches have been used to fight nazis?

In an abandoned oceanside hotel, a woman ties her man to the bed, blindfolds him and, consensually, begins to have sex with him. Before she can get far, she's quietly dispatched by an 18-inch puppet with a drill atop his head and her body is dragged away. Then, another woman climbs onto the bed to take her place. This woman is a bit shorter though. She's only 18 inches tall. She's a puppet too.

She teases the tied-up man's nipples playfully, letting him enjoy the moment a little longer, before opening her wooden jaws wide and hawking up a big, black leech. The process seems stressful, painful to her, but she does her work, deploying one leech after the next upon her bound victim. The leeches writhe as they make their way out of her mouth. So goes one of the most bizarre kills in all of horror filmdom, a fitting introduction to Leech Woman.

1989's *Puppet Master*, the first film in the series, opens in 1939. Inside the hotel, the Bodega Bay Inn, a puppet runs through the halls. We see the world from his point of view as he tries to stay out of sight of hotel guests. He seems as scared of people as they are of him. At one point, he catches an elderly lady by surprise. She screams and throws up her arms. In reaction, he also screams and throws up his arms. This is the puppet known as Blade, wrapped in a black trench coat, his skull-like face hiding under a black fedora.

He is afraid of something far more sinister than hotel guests though. Blade is in a hurry to warn Andre Toulon that nazi assassins have arrived at the hotel. Toulon, the puppet master of the film's title, comforts Blade, promises to protect him and the other puppets. Then, before the nazis can find him and do their job, Toulon pulls out a pistol and kills himself.

Flash forward to present day and we find a man waking from a horrible daydream of leeches, the first hint of the horrors to come. This is Alex, an anthropologist who can see the future in his dreams. He is summoned to the Bodega Bay Inn to join a group of psychics. They have been called there by Neil, another psychic, who awaits them in his casket, having recently killed himself.

The puppets start picking off the psychics one-by-one as they work quickly to unravel the mystery of what is going on and learn Toulon's secrets. Unfortunately, Neil found the puppets first. He discovered them and their reanimating serum when he was renovating the hotel. And he does not have positive intentions. He's sick of experimenting on the puppets. Now, he's killing humans so he can use Toulon's knowledge to experiment with reanimating them, as he has reanimated himself.

When the puppets get wind that Neil plans to use

the remaining serum on his collection of dead psychics instead of on them, their loyalty disappears. They turn on him, working together on one final kill. Blade uses his hook to pry Neil's mouth open, allowing Leech Women to spit a large and nasty leech down his throat. The rest of the puppets join in on the bloodshed. Teamwork!

The most well-known of the bloodsucking leeches are the medicinal leeches, which were historically used by medical practitioners to treat a variety of maladies (and are still used by hospitals today in limited circumstances). These are the leeches the killer puppet known as Leech Woman spits onto her victims, though, obviously, she has no intention of healing them.

Leech Woman's evolution as a character began with a vague idea of killer puppets from producer Charles Band. He turned the idea over to concept artist Lee MacLeod, who brought the idea to life as a poster. This was a common practice for Band at the time. He'd brainstorm ideas and have artwork created before a script had been written. Then he'd take the posters to distributors and see which ones they were interested in. Whichever films sold to distributors would be the ones he ultimately produced.

MacLeod's art did not include Leech Woman. She didn't become a character until Kenneth J. Hall wrote the script. However, the version of her in the script was dramatically different than the one that made it to the screen. In the book *Puppet Master Complete*, Hall describes his vision: "My puppet had a body of clear glass with a metal forked tongue to drain people's blood."

When director David Schmoeller was brought in to direct the film, he insisted on rewriting the script, changing Leech Woman in the process. Visual effects supervisor and puppet animator David Allen and his team interpreted the updated script to produce the leech-barfing femme fatale seen in the film.

David Allen is a legend of stop-motion animation. Like many special effects artists, he started DIY, making his own stop-motion movies before moving into low-budget films like *The Crater Lakes Monster* and *Laserblast,* an early Charles Band film. He eventually moved on to bigger budget movies like *Batteries Not Included* and *Young Sherlock Homes.* Unlike some special effects artists though, he never left the realm of low-budget films entirely, continuing to work on *Puppet Master* and other Charles Band projects for Full Moon Productions.

Leech Woman, as well as the other puppets, was brought to life with traditional rod puppetry, which is the style of puppetry where thin wooden or metal rods are used to move the puppet's limbs, as well as animatronics, which is when the puppet is controlled mechanically by remote. It's the stop-motion animation by David Allen and his team, however, for which Leech Woman and the rest of the puppets are best known. This is despite the fact that only a few minutes of stop-motion animation ended up on the screen.

Puppet Master is often dismissed as low-budget shelf fodder from the days of the video store, but there's a reason it's a cult favorite. This direct-to-video flick starts wild and rarely lets up, and the sequels turn the weirdness dial up further and further with each entry.

Puppet Master 2 (1990) opens in a foggy cemetery. Leech Woman stands at the edge of an open grave, looking down as another puppet finishes uncovering the coffin of Andre Toulon. The puppets pour the reanimating serum onto him and he comes to life, his rotting arms reaching up into the night sky.

Later, a group of paranormal researchers converge on Bodega Bay Inn to die. I mean, ummm, to conduct research. They have heard about the events of the first movie, and they want to find out what happened. One of them, a pop psychic who authors corny articles predicting alien attacks, declares about the hotel that "a taint of unholy fury has been absorbed by every particle of this place." She's not wrong.

While our researchers get to researching, the reanimated Toulon is hidden away elsewhere in the Inn, building a new puppet. He's wrapped in white bandages like a mummy, which he more or less is since he's been dead more than half a century at this point. He wears a fancy black suit. It becomes clear quickly that this is not the doting puppet master of the first film. The goodness must have rotted out of his brain after all those years in his coffin.

He commands the puppets to kill the researchers and collect their "digeneral lobes," which he needs to make more serum. Despite there being no such part of the brain as a digeneral lobe, the puppets are surprisingly successful in retrieving them. Though Torch, the new puppet, who has a blowtorch for a hand, accidentally burns a few of them. This prompts the puppets to try to sneak in some digeneral lobes from pigs from a nearby farm, but those won't do the trick.

Initially, Toulon is making the serum to keep his puppets, and himself, alive. Until he discovers that Carolyn, one of the researchers, is the spitting image of his dead wife, Elsa. Then he changes his strategy. He builds two life-size puppets, one that looks like him and one that looks like Elsa. He kidnaps Carolyn, kills himself, and moves his soul into the puppet version of himself.

Once again, the puppets find themselves betrayed by a master who wants to use the serum for himself instead of sharing it with them. They turn on him and kill him. Carolyn escapes in the process, but the puppets don't let the full-size Elsa puppet go to waste. They find the body of their first victim, the alien predictor psychic lady, and shift her soul into the Elsa puppet so she can drive them around.

Leech Woman's first kill of the movie is also her last. She sneaks up on a couple hog farmers who live near the Inn. She catches them sleeping, easily offing the husband in his slumber. Disappointingly, she uses a tiny knife. No leeches are deployed. What is the point of having the ability to hork out killer leeches if you're not going to use it?

The wife wakes up and screams, but she's not as easy a target as her husband. She grabs her shotgun and gets to stalking Leech Woman through the shadows of the farmhouse. She takes a shot and misses, then trades her shotgun for a cast-iron frying pan.

Leech Woman is not a great hider. She's doing a weird giggle moan the whole time. She climbs onto the mantel and pushes a doll off. The toy lands in front of the farm lady, shattering on the floor. The farm lady cries out and falls to her hands and knees to collect the pieces. She shows more emotion over the loss of this toy than her husband.

Truly angry now, she mashes Leech Woman with her frying pan, stomps her, then throws her into the woodburning stove, giving Our Lady of Leeches an unceremonious end.

Leech Woman's death was no random act. At the time, Charles Band's Full Moon Productions had a distribution deal with Paramount Pictures, one of the biggest film studios in the world. Full Moon made the films. Paramount helped get them out to the video rental stores that ate them up. To an extent, Full Moon was beholden to Paramount and, unfortunately, Paramount's execs were no fun. According to Band's commentary on the blu-ray release, the execs thought Leech Woman was too gross, so they pressured Band to kill her off. He did as requested, but she wouldn't go away easily.

Puppet Master 3 (1991) makes up for the lack of Leech Woman action in the previous film, and undermines Paramount's request to get rid of her. On the surface, it is the story of the puppets' origin, but it's Leech Woman's story at heart, and a love story too—love and revenge.

The film opens on a nazi flag waving in Berlin, 1942. Under orders from Hitler, a doctor is conducting a gruesome experiment. He's trying to create a "death corps," a team of zombie soldiers to take bullets on the frontlines of World War II. So far, his experiments have been unsuccessful, and he's getting pressure from his superiors to deliver results.

Cut to Andre Toulon's theater, where the puppet master is putting on a show in front of a large group of kids. In this show, the gunslinging cowboy puppet known as Six Shooter shoots a cowering Hitler puppet. Backstage after the show, Toulon and his wife Elsa show their beloved puppets to a small group who marvel at how alive the puppets seem.

A nazi goon shows up, also intrigued by the puppets. He warns Toulon to change the subject matter, but Toulon argues it's merely a puppet show. On his way out, the nazi peers through the window and sees the puppets moving on their own, as Toulon administers shots of his lifegiving serum to each of them.

That night, Toulon gifts Elsa a puppet he has created in her image, a beautifully carved toy with an elaborate white dress and black hair in a perfect updo. He confesses that he had tried to paint her portrait, but it never looked good enough. So he instead turned to the art he was more familiar with. The two share their love for each other, with Elsa declaring she will never leave Toulon.

Meanwhile, the nazi goon reports Toulon to his leaders, and the nazis conspire to attack the dissident. They storm Toulon's theater, kidnap him, take the puppets, and kill a defiant Elsa in the process. Of course, the puppets fight back. They attack and kill the nazis. With this first slaughter of nazis, the puppets become the true heroes of the story.

Toulon makes his way back to the ruins of his theater, which the nazis have burned down. On the destroyed shelves, he finds a jar full of medical leeches. Almost cheerfully, he declares, "Leeches? You'll suck their life's blood away."

He leads the puppets to the morgue and retrieves Elsa's corpse. He places her essence into her puppet avatar and brings her back to life in puppet form. "Elsa," he says, "this is the best I can do for you now." Pulling a leech out of the jar, he adds, "But you can still revenge yourself."

He drops a leech into her mouth, and her puppet body quakes. It changes her. Her neat updo of long black hair comes down. A purple hue comes over her face. The peaceful expression Toulon so lovingly carved for her turns to one of horror. Does she want this?

Later in the film, Toulon explains that the secret ingredient that makes his serum work on his subjects is the desire not only to live, but to get vengeance. All the souls that inhabit his puppets have two things in common, Elsa included: they were all killed by nazis, and they all want to kill nazis.

This marks a significant difference from other mad scientist movies, like *The Bride of Frankenstein* and its descendants. In those films, the subjects are always unwilling. They, mostly women, are brought back to life or experimented on either for the vanity or needs of the men who have chosen them as their subjects. Not here. Leech Woman is alive because she wants to be alive.

And she wants to kill nazis.

Her first target is the goon who initially tattled on Toulon. She and the rest of the puppets find him, on his own, trying to fix his broken-down car. Her moans are almost sexual as she climbs on top of the nazi to slowly choke a stream of leeches onto his face.

Now in full makeup, Elsa is clad in a ruby dress, matching scarf, and a glittery top. I wonder, did Elsa change her clothes on her own? Possibly, but I imagine Toulon lovingly sewing a new wardrobe for his wife, one still beautiful, but more suitable for her new incarnation as a femme fatale. Her white, innocent, almost-bridal dress she first wore needed to be placed with one in a color that doesn't show bloodstains.

Behind the scenes, the reason for Leech Woman's wardrobe change was more practical. Chris Endicott, who worked on the puppet crew, explains:

> The biggest challenges Leech Woman provided were her design and her dress in *Puppet Master 1* and *2*. Because she was modeled as a human-ish figure, and not as puppet-like as the others, her movements needed to be as realistic as we could get. And her first dress made it harder to hide the puppeteering rods and special rigs we used with the others. She got two new costumes in *Puppet Master 3*, and they

made it much easier to hide those devices, and get better control of her performance.

From here, it's cat and mouse, with the nazis hunting Toulon and his puppets, while they become nazi hunters, picking off their enemy one-by-one, fulfilling their reason for existence.

They take up residence in a blown-up building, perhaps an old warehouse. It serves for a while, but the nazis eventually find Toulon's hiding space. Elsa and the puppets narrowly escape with Toulon. They make it back to the ruins of his theater.

The bloody finale sees Toulon and the puppets slaughtering the last of the nazis, killing the nazi leader who has been hunting them. Then they flee the country, heading to Switzerland, and maybe, eventually, America.

Before this happens though, there is a tender scene where Toulon collapses on a bench back at his theater, exhausted. Elsa climbs up next to him, gently brushes his hair out of his face with her little wooden hand and comforts him. It's a wonderful scene near the end of the film that shows how strong the bond is between these two lovers, how it transcends flesh and mortality.

Puppet Master 3 is easily the best of the series, and its path to the screen was interesting. In early 1990, soon after the release of the first movie, Full Moon Productions teamed up with Malibu Graphics and its subsidiary Eternity Comics to publish a series of comic books based on their films. First up would be an adaptation of the first *Puppet*

Master film. However, the writer, David de Vries, refused to do the job unless given liberty to expand the story beyond the film. Everyone agreed, and he was unleashed.

What de Vries created was an adaptation that went far deeper into Andre Toulon's history than the film did. Then, when it came time to make the third film, the screenwriters took inspiration from the lore de Vries had created for the comics, pulling some elements scene for scene. It was the comic that introduced the entire World War II plot, turning the puppets into nazi fighters, which was only hinted at in the first film. It was the comic that introduced Leech Woman as Elsa's reincarnation.

There are differences though. There's a particularly disturbing scene in the comic where Leech Woman sneaks up on a nazi while he is driving. He is unaware of her presence until he feels something below his waist. A shocked expression comes over his face. He looks down to find his fly open, and Leech Woman, face down, unleashing her pets within.

Despite having such a pivotal role in the third film, Leech Woman sadly becomes scarce in the following films. She's absent from parts 4 and 5, presumably because they take place chronologically after part 2, in which she died a fiery death. Inexplicably though, she returns in the sixth film, *Curse of the Puppet Master*, where she and the puppets have been purchased at auction by a new puppet master and his daughter. Even here though, she is mostly in the background and has no kill scenes.

The seventh film, *Retro Puppet Master*, attempts to

build on, or rather in front of, *Puppet Master 3.* This is the story of young Toulon and how he discovered the secret of animating his puppets. More importantly, it is the story of the first meeting between Toulon and Elsa, who would later become Leech Woman. Sadly, her role is as little more than bait for some ghouls to catch Toulon. Gone is the defiant Elsa of *Puppet Master 3*, replaced by a generic damsel in distress, saved by dashing young Toulon. There is no Leech Woman action either.

Leech Woman is scarce or absent from the next couple films. Thankfully, she returned for *Puppet Master: Axis of Evil.* At this point, the series gets back to what it does best: showing puppets killing nazis.

Axis of Evil picks up where the introduction to the first film left off. After Toulon kills himself to avoid capture by the nazis, a young woodworker employed at the hotel finds the puppets. Thus begins a tale of intrigue about American agents fighting nazi spies in the shadowy backstreets of 40s Los Angeles.

Leech Woman only gets one good scene in this entry of the series, but it might be her most disgusting. She is sent to kill a Japanese spy. She locates him quietly eating a plate of sushi in the back room of the theater he and his fellow spies are using as their base of operations. She climbs onto a balcony above him. When he's not looking, she retches one of her leeches onto his plate. Not noticing it, the spy eats it, sending him into blood-spewing contortions and eventual death.

The next movie, *Axis Rising*, marks Leech Woman's

last appearance in the series as of now. Thankfully, she goes out in style. The film continues the story of U.S. agents trying to rid Los Angeles of nazi spies. This time though, the nazis have taken it up a notch. They've found a puppet master of their own, who creates a team of nazi puppets. The first created is Bombshell, a blonde in a nazi hat with a mostly unbuttoned white blouse revealing big metal breasts that flip down to uncover a pair of machine guns. Sure, perhaps these are more practical weapons than a mouthful of killer leeches, but where's the wow? Where's the romance?

She and her fellow nazi puppets are sent to track down the American puppets, now firmly the heroes of the story, commencing a new game of cat and mouse (or puppet and puppet). The budget for this film is dramatically lower than the first few. The special effects are crude. But the all-out battle between the American and nazi puppets at the climax is a hoot, complete with Leech Woman slapping the heck out of Bombshell in a rolling-around, all-out puppet babe brawl. It almost makes up for the near total lack of leech killings. Almost. Of course, the American puppets send the nazi puppets packing. In the finale, the nazi puppets turn on and attack the nazis. Turns out they were made with the souls of people the nazis killed, so they don't have the loyalty the nazis had expected. And the ranks of good killer puppets increases.

Unfortunately, the three films that follow do not include Leech Woman. It's a sad state of affairs for one of the coolest female monsters of all time. Maybe someday she will get her due. But back to leeches! Now that you know about how our prehistoric friends sucked the life out of nazis, how do you feel about them?

THE BEASTS OF BEAUTY

There is a monster that stalks all women from birth till death. It is persistent, unavoidable, and terrifying. It whispers to us that we are not pretty enough, not young enough, not good enough. This monster is, of course, the female beauty norm—the societal expectation that we be young and pretty.

In the article "The Beauty Myth" from the *Journal of Personality and Social Psychology*, scholars Leeat Ramati-

Ziber, Nurit Shnabel, and Peter Glick point out that in America alone, women spend an average of 45 minutes a day trying to make ourselves pretty. Our spending accounts for almost all the $115-billion-annually beauty product industry. When we fail to meet beauty norms, we face discrimination at work and elsewhere. These norms are a means of maintaining the patriarchy. As the article puts it, "In an age of increasing secularization, the female beauty norm replaced orthodox religious values such as chastity as an alternative way to control women."

This tool of controlling women, and our reaction to it, is the focus of Coralie Fargeat's 2024 film, *The Substance*, which features a Golden Globe Award–winning performance by Demi Moore as Monstro Elisasue, a gloopy, fleshy representation of the harm women suffer trying to adhere to beauty norms, and one of the coolest monsters to grace the silver screen in ages, not to mention the yuckiest.

The Substance opens with the creation of Elisabeth Sparkle's star on the Hollywood Walk of Fame, then time lapses on it as it is forgotten and falls into disrepair. Cut to Elisabeth filming an 80s-style aerobics video. As she guides viewers through the moves, she says, "Think about those bikini bods. You wanna look like a giant jellyfish on the beach?" Finished filming, she walks away from the set as people wish her happy birthday. She's 50 years old.

Later, over dinner, she meets with Harvey, the producer of her show. He lets her know that her time is up and she is being replaced. He's a gross, lecherous slob—an easy avatar for the mechanisms that foist these beauty standards onto society, and on women in particular. He demands his staff find a young and hot replacement for Elisabeth.

Elisabeth gets in a minor car accident on her way home. At the hospital, she is surreptitiously given a flash drive with information about The Substance, which promises not only a younger, more beautiful version of herself, but a better, more perfect version. She orders her first kit, which requires navigating to a bizarre, hidden room of delivery boxes. She picks up her kit, brings it home, and begins.

The Substance causes Elisabeth to birth Sue through a slit along her spine. As promised, Sue is a younger, more beautiful version of Elisabeth. Sue will exist for seven days before she must switch her consciousness back to her Elisabeth body, who then gets her allotted seven days. The Substance comes with a warning that this timeframe must be strictly followed.

Fawned over by Harvey, Sue immediately gets Elisabeth's old job. The two women then go back and forth, with Elisabeth mostly sitting around her fancy apartment while Sue uses her time to have fun, have sex, and build her career as Harvey's newest aerobics-instructing sensation.

The film strains to use the least flattering lighting and angles to accentuate every flaw on Elisabeth's body. A striking shot of her sitting alone at a shadowy bar in a slit-back evening gown is engineered to show every wrinkle and fold of flesh on her back. Are these flaws that Elisabeth, as a character, perceives? There is a moment prior to her taking her first injection where she stands in front of a mirror, examining her naked body. She doesn't seem to dislike it. Her expression isn't one of self-hate. It's resignation more than anything. It isn't how she feels that's motivating her to take this injection. It's how she's treated in an industry where she was once the star.

Sue, on the other hand, enjoys her body. She gets a similar mirror scene, where she runs her hands all over herself excitedly. Sue gets the most flattering angles and lighting, and scene after scene show her being young and pretty, hammering in the idea, trying hard to make you think young and pretty people are better. See how she shuts the fridge with her nubile butt? See how she drinks soda with her voluptuous mouth? So much better! You start to wonder what point the film is arguing.

Soon, Sue starts taking more than her allotted seven days. When she does, Elisabeth is further aged upon revival. The first time results in a hideously wrinkled, corpse-like index finger which she tries to wash off. All the while, the mysterious makers of The Substance respond to complaints from both Elisabeth and Sue with reminders that they are the same person.

After Sue steals so much time, Elisabeth is left a hunched, elderly mess. Elisabeth calls to terminate the program. This requires her to inject a syringe full of black serum into Sue's heart while she is unconscious. She begins to do so but stops short. "I hate myself," she says. She successfully revives Sue, who upon seeing that Elisabeth tried to terminate her, attacks. Sue brutally beats Elisabeth to death before she realizes that if one dies, they both die.

But they don't die easy.

Sue makes her way to the studio, where she's been promoted to host the big New Year's Eve show. When she gets there, she begins falling apart. First, she loses a tooth. Then she loses more teeth. Then an ear. So begins one of the wildest parades of grotesqueries ever seen in film.

Desperate, she tries to use The Substance to create the promised younger, prettier version of herself. As expected when making a copy of a copy, the results are not so great. The new body that emerges is a twisted collection of tumorous lumps and folded flesh. She has a melted version of Sue's face on her head, while Elisabeth's visage is on her back. Limbs emerge hither thither. Eyeballs are randomly placed. She has a single shock of black hair, which she hilariously burns off trying to curl with a curling iron.

This is Monstro Elisasue, and she is not giving up yet! She pokes some earrings into random earless spots and smears on some makeup. Not getting the hoped-for results from her beautification, she instead affixes a picture of Sue to her head and slathers some extra lipstick on it.

Good enough! She proceeds to stage and takes her place among her topless, Las Vegas-style backup dancers. When her Sue mask falls off, the crowd is stunned. A fissure opens in her flesh and she excretes a breasticle that plops to the floor. The crowd turns on her. "A monster! A freak!" Some flee, while others charge the stage to beat her.

"It's just me," she cries, but it's not enough to stop a man from bashing her head off. Thankfully, she sprouts a new one. Her blood sprays everywhere. Crowd members slip on it as they run away, screaming.

Monstro Elisasue eventually escapes amidst the panic. Running from the theater, she falls to pieces on the sidewalk. Eventually, all that's left is Elisabeth's face, which slopulates back to where the film began, her Walk of Fame star. When she reaches it, she completely dissolves.

In this film, the special effects are amazing, and emphasize old-fashioned, practical techniques such as prosthetics rather than CGI. As fun as the effects are though, every minute of The Substance is heavy-handed. There's even a scene that literalizes the oft-repeated, guilty-eating phrase, "This is going straight to my ass." The day after Elisabeth eats a chicken wing, the wing pops out of Sue's butt. Harvey, that avatar for all that is bad about men, tells Sue to smile at one point. "Pretty girls should always smile!" he says, before she starts losing her teeth. The film is so free of nuance it makes Pixar look subtle. Pixar is a good comparison, actually. With all its primary colors and bold letters, *The Substance* is like a big, oozy cartoon.

To be fair, Demi Moore's performance does have nuance. She's the heart of the movie, saying more with a glance than any of the in-your-face dialogue could ever hope to convey. I grew up watching movies like *Street Trash* and *The Toxic Avenger*—oozy, gooey slopfests that *The Substance* fits in with nicely, and it's wild to see a film of this ilk with A-list actors.

In a sense, this feels like a full-circle moment for

Moore. She began her career in B-movies. One of her first roles was in Charles Band's 1982 postapocalyptic sci-fi film *Parasite*, in which she tangled with a creature that pops out of peoples' guts. Around the same time, she—or rather her backside—appeared on the poster for one of the most notorious rape-revenge films of all time, *I Spit on Your Grave*. While her image is now synonymous with the film, she was not actually in it.

Moore's Golden Globe win for her performance in *The Substance* is a win for sloppy horror movies and their fans. This is the first time an actor has won a Golden Globe for playing a monster in makeup. In fact, the only other time an actor has won a notable award for such a role was when Fredric March tied for best actor in 1932 for his dual role as Dr. Jekyll and Mr. Hyde. It's almost hard to believe that a movie with multiple scenes of DIY, pus-riddled spinal taps that serve no purpose other than grossing viewers out won a dang Golden Globe. What a time to be alive!

As a darkly humorous body horror jam, it gets an A+.

As a feminist treatise about the destructiveness of female beauty standards, however, it fails miserably. In trying to make a statement against beauty standards, *The Substance* makes the definitely-not-feminist move of punishing the woman for wanting to meet them.

We all know beauty standards can be harmful and, for many of us, unattainable. But *The Substance* hinges on this ultimatum that either you stop trying to adhere to beauty standards and risk your livelihood, your romantic prospects, your general treatment as you move around in the world, or you do adhere to them and get turned into a mutant pile of meat glop.

Where is the punishment for the men whose actions support these standards? In *The Substance,* Harvey is portrayed as a slob, but he's a successful slob who suffers only the failure of his New Year's Eve show. If anyone should have been turned into a glop pile, it's him. And how about the punishment for the medical and cosmetics industries? For the culture as a whole? Why do women have to bear this weight? You wouldn't make an anti-capitalist movie and punish a character for going to work, right?

But what a gooey, glorious punishment it is. I'm putting a lot of weight on director Coralie Fargeat. In general, women filmmakers are held to a higher standard than male filmmakers, especially in the horror genre, and that's not fair. Women should not be required to make films with feminist meanings, or any meanings at all, really. Women are pressured to make art with meaning, while men can make a meaningless gloopfest and everyone high-fives.

That said, in interview after interview about the film, Fargeat hammered home that she was trying to make a message movie. In an interview with *Vogue,* she says, "Your image defines you and your self-worth. But I thought that if I could create something meaningful about these issues, it could also serve as a form of liberation." I don't think it's liberating to see a woman destroyed for trying to meet the prescribed beauty norm and keep her job.

The interviewers themselves are part of the problem,

reflecting how women are held to a higher standard. All the questions are about meaning and symbolism, trying to be deep. It's the wrong approach. What should be celebrated here is how Fargeat created one of the grossest body horror movies of all time, while injecting the most subversive sense of humor possible. The breasticle eruption scene I mentioned at the climax of the film is timed so perfectly to elicit a gut-busting laugh—if you are willing to let yourself, if you are willing to accept that you have waded into this mess and, yes, that at this exact moment, the pinnacle of this woman's long and illustrious career, first as Elisabeth, then as Sue, now as the stunningly wretched Monstro Elisasue—you realize nothing more awkwardly funny could happen than this perfect, disturbing, sickening, fleshy thing.

That's what interviewers should have been discussing with the director, this mining of the darkest, most fluid-filled humor, where men, let alone women, rarely tread. Instead, they ask their pretentious Pixar questions about what it all means, which is obvious even if your eyeballs are arranged like Monstro Elisasue's. That meaning is simple and corny and wrong and that's okay, because it doesn't need to be anything more. Liberation indeed!

While *The Substance* is the wildest, it's not the first movie to turn a woman into a monster because she committed the sin of trying to stay youthful and pretty. Monstro Elisasue comes from a long line of similarly contorted women's bodies, starting with *The Wasp Woman* in 1959.

Directed by legendary B-movie maker Roger Corman,

The Wasp Woman opens with Janice Starlin, owner and figurehead of cosmetic brand Janice Starlin Enterprises, as she berates a conference room full of her employees for the company's decline in sales. A brash employee blames the decline on the fact that Janice's face is no longer appearing in ads.

"There's only one small problem you've overlooked," she replies. "Not even Janice Starlin can remain a glamour girl forever." She's not even sad about it. She is a powerful, graceful leader, regardless of her age. It's only her male employees who have an issue. But alas, the problem of declining sales remains. A business needs to sell its products.

Enter Dr. Zinthrop, a scientist who comes to Starlin with promises of a way to provide 10 to 15 years of rejuvenation. His substance is made from enzymes extracted from wasps. The wasps are played by honeybees, a casting decision that would make any entomologist cringe.

Interestingly, there's an element of scientific truth to using honeybees in this way. Scientists have found that honeybee venom has an anti-aging effect in that it reduces wrinkles. A number of bee venom face creams are now on the market. Wasp venom hasn't been found to have the same properties. Certainly though, *The Wasp Woman* is a better title for a horror flick than *The Honeybee Woman*, so let's give the filmmakers the benefit of the doubt. (I live on a farm where I grow native plants to encourage dwindling pollinator populations, primarily bees and wasps. As a result, I tend to get stung at least once a year. Fingers crossed some of the anti-aging impacts come through!)

Speaking of animal-related casting decisions, the scene where Zinthrop proves the effectiveness of his serum to Starlin might be one of the most hilariously poorly thought-out sequences in B-movie history. If you're a fan of B-movies, you know the competition for that title is fierce. Zinthrop injects the serum into an elderly guinea pig. We know it is elderly because it is dirty and its fur is mussed up. Starlin begs Zinthrop to put the animal out of its misery. But with the serum injection, the guinea pig becomes young again. Did the filmmakers replace the previous guinea pig with a young guinea pig to demonstrate this? No. Did they clean the dirt spots off and comb its fur to give the impression of newfound youth? No? Instead, they cut to a young rat. Starlin marvels! The serum works! I wonder, did Corman simply think the audience would not be able to tell one rodent from the next? Or did he not know the difference? Likely, that's all there was at the nearest pet shop, so he winged it.

Janice soon starts taking injections. There is some progress, but she doesn't think it's fast enough. Meanwhile, her employees think Zinthrop is a scammer, trying to fleece Janice. With this pressure, she starts sneaking extra injections against Zinthrop's orders. It works. She becomes young and beautiful again, to her employees' awe. Janice calls a meeting about bringing this age-defying product to the market and rejuvenating Janice Starlin Enterprises in the process.

Of course, this miracle substance comes with side effects. At night, Janice turns into the Wasp Woman, buzzing around the office, attacking her employees and sucking blood from their throats, before reverting to her human form during the day.

As the Wasp Woman, she has the head of a wasp on a human body. With big, segmented eyes, reaching antennae and a furry face, she stalks the office halls (even though wasps don't have fur). As cheap as the mask looks, it is also inexplicably cool when paired with the black turtleneck and dangling necklaces she wears, giving an insectoid beatnik vibe.

Oddly enough, the onscreen wasp woman design is the opposite of the Wasp Woman presented on the iconic film poster, in which she is depicted with a wasp body and a human's head. Together, the poster and the onscreen version likely inspired the song "Queen Wasp" by the horror punk band The Misfits. "Vampire girl gonna strike to kill," the lyrics begin, referencing the way the Wasp Woman sucks the blood from the throats of her victim. Never mind that wasps don't actually suck blood.

Her killing spree continues until Zinthrop throws acid into her face and she falls from a window to her death. The penultimate scene of her acid-melted body lying dead on the concrete is ahead-of-its-time disgusting, and an appropriate precursor to the ending of *The Substance.* Finally, the film cuts to a shot of honeybees buzzing in their nest. Well, we're supposed to think they're wasps. Whatever!

The Wasp Woman was Susan Cabot's last role, following a decade-plus career that saw her starring in a variety of westerns and adventure films. It was after her acting career though that her life took some truly wild turns. In 1959, she was enlisted by the CIA to "entertain" Jordan's King Hussein. Documents declassified in 2018 revealed she was one of several women the CIA set the monarch up with while he was visiting Los Angeles.

The former actress and the monarch ended up being together for a brief time. Cabot gave birth to a son in 1961. Though the monarch never acknowledged the child was his, it was later discovered that Jordan was making regular payments to Cabot that appeared to be child support.

On December 10, 1986, Cabot was killed in her Los Angeles home. Her killer was her son, 22-year-old Timothy Scott Roman, who had been subjected to a lifetime of experimental medical treatments overseen by his mother. In court, Roman's defense attorney said, "Mr. Roman is probably, really, an experiment of the human race."

At an early age, doctors found that Roman wasn't producing growth hormone and was not growing. At his mother's behest, he was treated for 15 years with an experimental hormone later discontinued when it was linked to neurological disorders in some patients.

In the 1950s, scientists began treating growth hormone deficiencies in children with human growth hormone (HGH) extracted from cadavers. This wasn't a particularly common treatment. An article from *Genetics Unzipped* indicates it was used on about 27,000 kids from the 50s through 1985, when it was discontinued. Unfortunately, Cadaveric Pituitary Extracted Human Growth Hormone was found to cause the fatal neurological disorder Creutzfeldt-Jakob disease. Scientists found CJD was passed from the corpses to the children.

While the evidence that HGH provides anti-aging properties to adults is slim and the FDA has not approved its use for this purpose, there are many who believe it can help, and obtain it either legally from a doctor who prescribes it off-label (the medical term for a prescription given for reasons other than what it was intended for) or illegally. After discovering the CJD connection, scientists thankfully developed a synthetic HGH, so human brains aren't used anymore. But before 1985?

Susan Cabot noticed that while on this treatment, her son was not aging at the normal rate. According to her friend Kathleen Hughes, in an interview with the show *Mysteries & Scandals*, the former actress started taking the same treatment in hopes of maintaining her own youth. The experiment, which was eerily similar to that of her character in *The Wasp Woman*, ended when she died at the hands of her son.

1987's *Evil Spawn* began its life as an unofficial remake of *The Wasp Woma*n called *Deadly Sting*, helmed by 80s low-budget legend Fred Olen Ray. He didn't like how it was shaping up, so he moved into the producer chair and handed it over to Kenneth J. Hall. Unfortunately, what was handed over wasn't much, some ideas and a few minutes of footage, including a random monologue by horror movie vet John Carradine, which was originally recorded for a completely different film, called *Frankenstein's Brain.*

Where there's a will to make a nonsensical schlock film though, there's a way, and Kenneth J. Hall, then at the beginning of what would come to be an illustrious career (including writing the first draft of the first film in the previously discussed *Puppet Master* series), had the will.

"You're not as young as you used to be! All the big parts are going to girls in their twenties," says Hollywood agent Harry to his client, Lynn Roman. Lynn, played by Bobbie Bresee, is upset the only script she's gotten recently is for a low-budget film called *The She-Demons.*

Lynn thinks the role is beneath her. She wants a bigger part, in a bigger-budget movie. She hatches a plan to contact the director of an upcoming major production. Before she reaches out to him, she decides to make sure she's at her best. "It's time to renovate Lynn Roman," she declares. She's referring to getting her hair and nails done, but a mystery woman conveniently shows up offering a treatment that will help Lynn reverse the aging process.

"This sounds like something out of a bad science-fiction film," Lynn says. She doesn't want any part of it initially. She has good reason to push back. Not only is the treatment experimental and unbelievable, but she likes her body. "You know," she explains, "it's not bad enough that people think I'm getting old, but I'm gonna tell the whole world that I owe my looks to some drug?" She rejects the offer. "This girl is all-natural ingredients. No preservatives added!"

The mystery woman leaves the serum behind anyway: two syringes of bright pink liquid. Lynn eventually gives in and injects herself. She projectile vomits immediately. What the mystery woman didn't disclose is what the serum is made of. No, it's not derived from wasps. This one is made from the guts of a weird space spider-rat creature. And it hasn't exactly been successfully tested.

The next day, Lynn wakes up looking much younger. She meets with the director of the major Hollywood production she is angling for the lead role in. They go out dancing and have a nice time together. When he brings her home, she gets up the courage to ask for the role. He gets angry and tells her she's too old, that the part is written for a woman in her twenties. She begs, but to no avail.

That night she mutates. Her shirt rips open, revealing an expanding brown exoskeleton where her skin used to be. She has glowing eyes, wriggling antennae, and bitey mandibles that twitch hungrily as she hunts her prey, buzzing. Despite having little screentime, her insectoid mutant form is incredibly cool and rises above the film's budget. Why have two mandibles when you can have a bunch? Why have short claws when you can have foot-long claws? It's a perfect example of the type of over-the-top monsters that were coming out of the 80s low-budget film boom.

The first victim of Lynn's massive claws is her secretary. She reverts to her human body in the daytime. At night, her buggy killing spree continues, and she takes out her cheating boyfriend, her agent, and more, while the man she's hired to co-write her autobiography desperately tries to save her.

He doesn't succeed. The cops eventually kill her before she can kill her biographer. Standing over her body, he says, "Vanity, that sin that caused the ancient gods to visit their punishment on man. That's what happened here." I don't think he knows anything about the ancient gods, and he clearly doesn't know anything about Lynn Roman either. Perhaps the more appropriate line would have been the line Carl Denham spoke as he stood over King Kong's body in Times Square: "It was beauty killed the beast." Or, more specifically, beauty norms and the expectations that come with them.

Lynn Roman's actions had nothing to do with vanity. Merriam-Webster defines vanity as "inflated pride in oneself or one's appearance." Lynn was proud of her appearance, but not excessively so. What happened here was the result of being pushed by beauty norms to desperately take steps to reclaim the career she had worked so hard for. So Lynn's biographer was way off when blaming vanity. I hope he gets fired from the job of writing Lynn's biography, because he doesn't get her at all.

Evil Spawn is a mess of a movie, but also a great example of the slapdash ways low-budget movies come together. often against all odds. Though, okay, saying *Evil Spawn* ever "came together" might be generous, but it was made, and released, and it's fun, and all of that is something.

1988's *The Rejuvinator* introduces another aging

starlet, Ruth Warren. Ruth is one of the primary funders of anti-aging research conducted by Dr. Gregory Ashton, and she's putting pressure on him to deliver. Complaining she hasn't had a good part in 30 years, she gives him an ultimatum: Either perform his procedure on her or she will cut off funding. "It's inhuman to allow a woman of my charm and ability to rot away in this ugly carcass," she complains.

On top of that, the doctor is getting pressure from the ethics committee, who think his practices are "unsound." He argues that his techniques have been used before. "Yes," the head of the ethics committee replies, "in concentration camps."

Up until this point, the ethics committee has been right. The last time the doctor tested his serum on a rat, the animal went feral and burst from his cage. He and his assistant finally get a stable result in the rat and figure that's good enough to move forward with using it on Ruth.

Of course, such serums are never made in normal ways. If you're not using wasp derivatives or ooze from space rat-spiders, then you've got to turn to a distillation of "the raw gray matter of the human brain," as the doctor does here. If you think, "My goodness, that is weird," remember the treatment *The Wasp Woman* actress Susan Cabot used on herself and her son in real life.

As for how our Dr. Gregory is getting his corpses, it turns out he is buying them from the black market for $1,000 each. According to Reuters, the cost for a corpse (non-black market) today is typically $3,000 to $5,000, though a good corpse could cost up to $10,000. (I imagine the black market cost is even more expensive now. Inflation hurts everyone.)

The doctor proceeds to give Ruth the serum. She becomes young and beautiful. Like in *The Substance*, the beautiful version of herself is played by a younger actress. She looks so different she concocts a new identity, Elizabeth. Much like Sue, Elisabeth Sparkle's younger alter ego in *The Substance*, she goes out and lives it up. She dances. She has sex. Though instead of having sex with some young guy, she inexplicably has sex with the doctor, despite having had no romantic affiliation prior.

But her youth doesn't last. She turns into a gooey mess and re-ages. "What is happening to me?" she screams, staring at the bathroom mirror.

"You're experiencing some complications," the doctor explains, which is a slight understatement.

With another round of injections, she's young again. She spends her days drinking wine and painting her nails, and her nights at clubs dancing and picking up dudes. When she re-ages next, it's not just a matter of getting old. Her skull expands. Her flesh gets mushy and distorted.

Thankfully, there are more injections to be had, but the whole experiment is jeopardized as the ethics committee tries to shut it down. Worse yet, the stream of corpses is starting to dry up. The shady guy who delivers them might be resorting to something worse than grave-robbing, though the doctor doesn't ask why the bodies have been warm lately.

Even knowing that each time she is young is limited, Elizabeth doesn't stop living. She goes to a rock and roll club to see the Poison Dollys. The Poison Dollys were an all-woman hard rock group from Long Island that were active throughout the 80s, releasing one self-titled album. They play a couple songs in the movie, "Turn Out the Lights" and "Nice Boy," which are perfect examples of fun, 80s hard rock, somewhere between metal and glam, and would fit in on a mixtape with Motley Crue and Poison.

If the scene seems particularly music video-esque, it's no coincidence. Director Brian Thomas Jones explains, "The idea was to get a music video out of it that we could intercut with scenes from the movie that would promote both the movie and the Dollys."

While the Poison Dollys play on stage, Elizabeth tries to pick up a guy on the dance floor. When she starts to change, she abandons him and makes her way to the bathroom. As she transforms, making icky noises, a couple of ladies doing drugs by the mirror complain, "You know, as soon as a club gets hot, they let in the bridge and tunnel crowd."

The next scene is my favorite. Elizabeth walks down a dark, empty New York City street. She is wearing a flowing white hooded cloak with white furry trim along the hood and cuffs, the kind you would expect on a Disney snow princess. With the hood pulled up, concealing her face, she could well be a snow princess, except for two things: 1) snow princesses do not gracefully glide through back alleys of 80s NYC, and 2) snow princesses do not have long, twisted, wiggling fingers reaching from the sleeves of their cloak. Even if they did, those fingers would not be used to kill a random woman in a phone booth and extract her brain.

Jones says the white cloak was "the kind of clothing an old movie star would have. In fact, it was specially constructed by our costume designer, Linda Lee Cocuzzo, because the hood had to fit over the very large monster prosthesis. All costumes for each scene were coordinated to match the downward spiral of Elizabeth's mental, emotional and physical condition."

Elizabeth sucks out the juices of her prey and then discards the brain, still beating, on the sidewalk. Do disembodied brains typically beat like hearts? I cannot confirm or deny, as my disembodied brain experience is limited, but it sure looks cool.

Elizabeth has turned full monster now. She removes her whimsical white hood to reveal her face. It is a disgusting, beautiful mess of jagged teeth, veins weaving in and out of twisted flesh, and a pile of brains stacked up on her head like the Bride of Frankenstein's beehive hairdo. It's blue and pink and glistening wet with old lady rage!

The doctor gets her back to the lab and gives her another injection, but he can't stop the cycle. Elizabeth transforms again and continues her killing spree, starting with the doctor's assistant, whose brain she gobbles up. When the doctor finally succeeds in synthesizing the serum so human brains are no longer needed to make it, it's too late. Elizabeth is happy to get what she needs straight from the source. "I don't need your serum anymore," she says.

After more murders, she realizes what she has become. "Help me," she begs the doctor. "End my suffering. I don't want to live like this anymore."

The doctor doesn't need to do anything though, as the brain-derived serum is not stable and Elizabeth/Ruth's body breaks down in a gooey explosion of spurting veins, blood, and pus. Her flesh melts and her face lands in a puddle on the floor, an ending *The Substance* would echo.

While the endings of *The Substance* and *The Rejuvenator* are quite similar, I'd be surprised if there was any intentional lifting of ideas, homage or otherwise. Despite being one of the most fun examples of 80s New York City B-movie filmmaking, *The Rejuvenator* is the most obscure of any I've covered in the book. It had a barely existent theatrical run on release before going to VHS and video store rental shelves in the late 80s. After that, it was only released on DVD in Germany. Even among fans of weird, obscure movies, this one is lesser known.

Jessica Dublin, the actress who played Ruth, the older version of the character, had a long career in B-movies reaching back to the 60s, including a number of European productions such as *Sex of the Witch* and *Death Has Blue Eyes.* According to Jones,

> I saw Jessica in the Troma *Toxic Avenger* movies. I thought she was a great character with a great over-the-top sense of humor, yet grounded enough to take this movie seriously. She reminded me of an aging screen star put out

> to pasture so when I was writing the script she immediately came to mind. She had such fun with the character and studied hard to affect the mannerisms of Ruth, and I think the transition between her and Elizabeth is very believable.

Vivian Lanko played Elizabeth, the younger version of the character. Jones says,

> I was part of a scrappy theatre group called 'Cucaracha.' We did off-off-Broadway productions, mostly experimental stuff, footing the bill for lofts and warehouses ourselves. Vivian was part of the group. She was a terrific actor with a lot of range and I knew she could pull off this part. She read the script and was all in.

It's stunning how similar these movies are. *The Substance*, as well as the others, has been compared to Oscar Wilde's classic novel, *The Picture of Dorian Gray*. There, a young man wishes to stay young and beautiful, and his wish is granted, while a portrait of him becomes old and ugly instead. In his everlasting youth, he engages in a life of sin and murder.

But comparing these films to Wilde's book is a misread of both. *The Picture of Dorian Gray* is about narcissism, and these films are not. Yes, all these women desire to be young and beautiful, but each is driven to that desire by external forces, mainly their careers. Their motivation is far more complex than simple narcissism. These movies are about how beauty norms shape our culture and force women to choose between taking steps to preserve our youth and beauty or accepting bodies that society tells us are no longer worth hiring, worth loving, worth anything.

The saying "beauty is in the eye of the beholder" is trash. We accept as a given that beauty is something bestowed on us and not innate, but it's not true. All of nature is beautiful. Our quest is not to earn it or achieve it, but to recognize what is already there against the roar of Hollywood and makeup ads. But even so, we exist in a world where we are perceived by others based on how we look, and their perceptions drive how they treat us.

And the reality is that it will always be easier to buy some creams or have some surgery than it will ever be to achieve an enlightened state of accepting we no longer have the same value, and it's certainly easier than extricating ourselves from societal beauty norms all together.

So I'll keep using my substances and I can only hope that if I'm punished for it, that my punishment comes in the form of becoming a wasp woman. That would be badass.

THE SNAKE-HAIRED WOMAN

Few femme monsters have been striking fear into the hearts of men as long as Medusa, the Gorgon. In mythology, Medusa's story is sparse and inconsistent, changing from one telling to the next, from one translation to the next. In turn, it has been interpreted many ways by modern academics.

Her first known written appearance was in Hesiod's poem *The Theogony.* Written around 700 BC, this poem tells the origins of the Greek gods. The tales of Greek gods all come from oral traditions, so her story was spoken long before that.

The version of Medusa's tale that has become the most popular, however, comes from the Roman poem *The Metamorphoses* by Ovid, which was written 1500 years later, in 800 AD. Roman and Greek mythology overlap quite a bit, and they have become intertwined in popular culture, though some names and stories differ. For the sake of consistency, I'll be using the Roman version of the myth of Medusa, but with the Greek names of gods, as that seems to be the most common, at least in pop culture.

Medusa was the most beautiful of three sisters. Words could not describe how pretty her hair was. Many would-be suitors longed for her, but Poseidon, the god of the sea, had sex with her. He picked the worst place to do it though—Athena's temple. Athena was so mad about this affront that she turned Medusa's lovely hair into snakes and cursed her to turn men to stone with a glance.

Even this telling is controversial. In Robert Graves's *Greek Gods and Heroes*, which retells the myth, Poseidon and Medusa merely kissed in Athena's temple. Translations of *The Metamorphoses* vary dramatically, though most present Poseidon as the aggressor. In some, he "seduced" Medusa. In others, he "ravished" her or "violated" her. In David Raeburn's and Horace Gregory's translations, among others, no punches are pulled: Poseidon raped Medusa.

The translation hinges on the Latin word *vitiasse*, which is what Ovid uses to describe the action Poseidon took upon Medusa. *Vitiasse* doesn't directly translate to "rape," but it could be interpreted to mean that, as the latter translators would argue. This is all subject to much debate among mythology nerds. Have modern translators interpreted the myth to fit their narrative? Was Ovid's retelling of Greek myths intended to make the gods look like scumbags? Should every mention of Medusa after *The Theogony* be discarded as impure? Can one version of a myth be right and another wrong?

Who cares? Arguing about what "really" happened in a myth is silly. None of it really happened. It's a story, and no iteration is more valid than the next. Okay, maybe Graves's version in which Medusa and Poseidon were smooching is a little less valid. Nonetheless, there's certainly no harm, and sometimes even strength, in finding meaning in a specific interpretation of a story.

In recent times, Medusa has become a patron saint of sexual assault survivors. In her essay "Ancient Gorgons: A Face for Contemporary Women's Rage," professor of religion and women's liberationist Emily Erwin Culpepper suggests Medusa is "one face of our own rage." Many women see themselves in the story of this woman who was raped by a man with social power and then punished for being a victim.

Let's face it, society doesn't treat sexual assault survivors well. Speaking up is as likely to result in public shaming, being called a liar, being called mentally ill, or being ostracized as it is in getting any form of justice. Whether she was raped or not, there was a power imbalance between herself and Poseidon, and even if the act is interpreted as consensual, she was not deserving of any curse.

Or was it a curse at all? The power to protect herself from men by turning them to stone is as easy to read as a gift as it is a curse. In fact, in some tellings of the myth, Athena herself used Medusa's visage on her shield as a form of protection. Many women, myself included, have Medusa tattoos, either for the same reason Athena put her visage on her shield or because of how the Gorgon's story mirrors their own as survivors of sexual assault.

1981's *Clash of the Titans* provides filmdom's most well-known representation of Medusa. Using *The Metamorphoses* as a starting point, it further develops the character. Though she has little screentime, she is central to the story, which begins as baby Perseus and his mother are thrown out to sea to die, only to be rescued by Zeus, who turns out to be Perseus's dad.

Zeus delivers them to their own idyllic island. There, they live in peace until Perseus hits adulthood. Then, the gods decide they have use for him. They steal him from the island and deposit him in the ruins of an amphitheater, where he is greeted by the poet Ammon and his gaggle of cats. Perseus wonders why he has been brought to this location. Ammon says, "The gods of Olympus are mysterious and their motives are erratic."

In one of the film's cutest moments, Ammon tells Perseus his island garb is not befitting someone like Perseus. Ammon retrieves a white robe he has been using as a cat blanket, though the cats are reluctant to let it go at first. Perseus graciously accepts. The gods give him a few additional, less fur-covered gifts: a sword, a shield with a mirrored inside, and a helmet of invisibility.

Which is great for him, because it turns out Perseus is a bit of a creeper. He uses the helmet to sneak into Andromeda's bedroom while she sleeps. Andromeda has been cursed by the devilish Calibos, who summons her dream self to visit him in his swamp home every night and prevents her from marrying until a man can answer a riddle. Watching Andromeda's body in bed, Perseus says, "Andromeda, I have found my destiny." Sure, he goes on to free her from her curse and promises to marry her, but sneaking into her room and watching her while she sleeps is still a stalker move, and the first of many reasons to dislike the so-called hero of this story.

Calibos's mom, the goddess Thetis, gets mad that Andromeda escaped her curse. She interrupts Perseus's and Andromeda's wedding, demanding Andromeda be sacrificed to the Kraken, a gigantic sea monster. That, of course, leaves our hero Perseus with no other option than to slay the Kraken.

Unfortunately, there's no how-to manual on slaying Krakens, so Perseus is sent to the Stygian Witches. These gals are an eyeless, bickering trio of cannibals constantly stirring their cauldron. They aren't immediately interested in offering free advice to this trespasser, but Perseus harasses them until they reveal that there is only one thing powerful enough to slay the Kraken: Medusa, or, more accurately, Medusa's head.

Medusa's gaze can turn men into stone. Her blood is poison. She's a bit of a recluse though, either because of the aforementioned qualities or because people keep trying to steal her head without bothering to ask if she'd like to help of her own volition.

Perseus gathers some warriors and travels to the Isle of the Dead. There, Perseus and his four soldiers make their way through a cave to the ruins of a temple. The sky here is blue and clear, though fog weaves around the crumbling pillars. The grounds are littered with the statues of men who have tried and failed to do what Perseus and his men have come to do.

Before they get a chance to die by Medusa's glance, however, the men are attacked by Cerberus, the massive, two-headed dog who guards the temple. Perseus slays the poor, mewling beast, but not before it takes out one of the men.

To sum up Perseus's heroic acts so far, he has snuck into one woman's bedroom to watch her sleep, harassed three elderly ladies, and killed a puppy. Two puppies, if you go by number of heads.

Into the temple the remaining men go, their faces hidden behind their shields in hopes of avoiding Medusa's gaze. It's not only her gaze they need to fear though. In a darkened room, fires burning in braziers and sconces cast shadows through which the Gorgon moves, not entirely in silence. She rattles her snake tail in warning at the trespassers, but they do not heed it.

Soon, they see the shadow of her head on a pillar, snakes writhing where her hair used to be. And is that a quiver of arrows on her back? An arrow in the back of one of Perseus's men serves to answer that question. If the arrow weren't enough to kill him, he falls face first into a puddle of acid.

Finally, Medusa emerges, pulling herself forward with her arms, staying close to the ground at first before rising up on her coiled snake's tail. She stands with a strong posture, shoulders drawn back. She is nude, covered in green scales, her expression one of pure anger. Despite still being outnumbered three to one, she does not retreat. Fearlessly, she nocks another arrow.

I love this depiction of Medusa. This Medusa is a warrior. She is monstrous, yes, but she is no victim, no tyrant. She is a woman holding her ground to protect the little space she has been allowed in this world of gods and men who see her as nothing more than a tool they can possess, and she has decorated her home with their hardened corpses.

This Medusa is the creation of Ray Harryhausen, often considered the master of stop-motion animation. *Clash of the Titans* was his last film, and truly the last bastion of stop-motion animation in a post–*Star Wars* world, a whimsical relic of older times. In a career that saw him breathe extraordinary life into a wide range of stop-motion dinosaurs, aliens, and, notably, an entire army of skeletons in *Jason and the Argonauts* (1963), Medusa may have been the pinnacle of his creations.

Though appearing taller than the humans who she battles in the film, Harryhausen's Medusa model was only a little over a foot tall in real life. All her movements were done by hand, frame by frame, and there were many to make.

Harryhausen explains in an interview with *American Cinematographer*: "For every frame of film, I had to move a snake into a different position. She had 12 snakes in her hair, plus the tails, plus her mouth moving, her eyes moved, her fingers moved, she shot an arrow and her tail rattled. She probably had over 100 joints in her body—150, perhaps—including the snakes."

The attention to detail is impeccable. The snakes on her head are all different colors and shapes. In addition to those, there is one solitary snake wrapped around her right forearm, acting as a makeshift living bracelet. It moves out of the way each time Medusa draws her bowstring back to fire.

Harryhausen deserves credit for his Medusa design, which combines elements of mythological depictions of Medusa with novel innovations like the snakelike body and archer motif, as well as for bringing her to life on screen through painstaking stop-motion animation. However, sculptor Janet Stevens, who sculpted the strong, serpentine, scaled body deserves some accolades too.

In the film, Medusa continues to even the odds. She nocks another arrow and strikes Perseus's last soldier. It's not a kill shot, but as the man crawls away he makes the mistake of looking back. Eyes wide and glowing green,

Medusa returns his gaze and he turns to stone.

Now there is only one trespasser left, though it's still not accurate to say the odds have been evened. After all, Perseus has the gods on his side, along with the sword and shield they have gifted him. The fight is fairer than it is in the original text of *The Metamorphoses* though, where he not-so-heroically sneaks up on Medusa while she and her snakes are sound asleep, cutting her head off without giving her a chance to fight back. Here, he tosses his shield so the inside will catch his own reflection. Medusa goes after it, thinking it is her foe. As she does, Perseus, lurking in the shadows, beheads her.

As her body writhes and her tail gives one last rattle, Perseus grabs her head by the now motionless snakes. He leaves the temple, emerging into the daylight, sword in one hand, her head in the next, an unearned expression of triumph on his face.

A famous sculpture by Benvenuto Cellini that was created in the mid-1500s captures this moment from the myth of Perseus as well. In 2008, the sculptor Luciano Garbati inverted the image in a statue of his own, which depicts Medusa carrying Perseus's severed head. Though the sculptor was not aware of Medusa's status as a feminist icon, the statue became famous as a symbol of the #MeToo Movement.

Though separated from her body, Medusa's role in *Clash of the Titans* is far from over. Away from the Isle of the Dead now, Perseus and some soldiers who were waiting for him to return from the island make camp. Sound asleep with Medusa's head in a sack swaying from a low-hanging branch of a nearby tree, their camp is invaded. The devilish Calibos appears. With his trident, he pierces the bag and Medusa's head in it. Drops of her blood fall to the sand. Each one turns into a giant scorpion. The men awaken and a battle ensues. The scorpions are killed, along with Calibos. Perseus loses more of his men, but he manages to stay alive and retains Medusa's head.

Perseus finds Pegasus, the winged horse, and flies back to Andromeda, arriving in the nick of time. She is chained to a cliff, awaiting sacrifice to the Kraken. As the Kraken rises from the sea, Perseus swoops in. The massive, many-armed sea creature knocks him off his flying horse and into the water with ease. Perseus swims to shore and, with the help of Bubo, a mechanical owl, recovers the bagged head of Medusa.

Atop the cliff, Perseus unbags the Gorgon's head. Clutching her by her writhing snakes, he holds her aloft. Her eyes glow green and turn the Kraken to stone. Andromeda is saved. The whole city is saved. Perseus tosses Medusa's head into the drink without so much as a thank-you.

The story of my Medusa tattoo, created with artist Jennifer Love, picks up at this point. In this telling, Medusa's snakes swim her to a nearby shore. They drag her back to her body. She sews herself back together, moves farther away from humankind, starts a garden of wildflowers, and creates a habitat for bumblebees, who buzz around her beloved snakes.

Not surprisingly, Italian cinema has been a hotbed of films based on Greek and Roman mythology, including no less than 25 movies about Hercules. In the wake of the success of *Clash of the Titans* and other sword and sorcery films, cult Italian director Luigi Cozzi made two Hercules films starring a well-oiled Lou Ferrigno, world-renowned bodybuilder and future star of *The Incredible Hulk* television series. The films are a charming vehicle for Ferrigno to flex his massive, glistening muscles, and he's a far more impressive hero than Harry Hamlin's Perseus. These Hercules films are also shameless in copying other films, particularly *Clash of the Titans.*

In the second of the Cozzi Hercules films, 1985's *The Adventures of Hercules*, the titular character must battle Medusa. The scene is similar to the battle between Perseus and Medusa in *Clash*, though with a noticeably lower budget. This stop-motion Medusa looks like a dollar store toy, with a bizarrely thin torso and overly long arms. It's as if the modelers built her a bit too short and to remedy the problem they pulled on her arms and legs and stretched her body out. She does come with one novel development though: the lower half of her body is that of a scorpion, complete with a stinging tail that lashes out at Hercules.

In all fairness, stop-motion animator Jean Manuel Costa deserves credit for this and many other stop-motion effects littered throughout the film. He obviously did not have a lot of money to work with, but nonetheless it is fun to watch. Scorpion Medusa doesn't get much screentime though. She's quickly killed by Hercules, who uses the same reflection-in-shield trick that Perseus used.

The best depiction of Medusa in Italian cinema, and the wildest interpretation of her ever, appears in Alberto de Martino's 1963 film, *Perseus Against the Monsters,* AKA *Perseus the Invincible,* AKA about 30 other titles.

There is no element of humanity in this version of Medusa. Here, she is a dark, lurching tangle of snakes with one big glowing orange eye in the middle that turns men to stone. She looks more like a god out of H. P. Lovecraft's imagination than anything out of Greek mythology.

As in other iterations of her story, she hasn't done anything to deserve her persecution. She's merely trying to live her own solitary life in a peaceful desert valley, but men keep coming to kill her and she keeps turning them to stone. She even has a dragon living in a pond near the entrance to her valley who tries to warn men not to come, but they come anyway. So now her valley is filled with hundreds of statues of soldiers. Which is why Perseus has come.

He has a war to fight with an army who wants to usurp his kingdom, so he needs an army of his own. He has been told that if he kills Medusa, the soldiers will awaken from their stone slumber, giving him an instant army.

Unfortunately, Perseus can't behead this Medusa, as she has no discernable head. It would be like trying to behead a tree. Instead, he stabs her in her glowing eye. As white muck oozes out all over her snakes, Perseus turns toward the statues. There is no movement. He cries out, again and again, "The Medusa is dead! You can awaken!" But they do not.

Perseus begins to despair, until finally the statues begin to move. Miraculously, despite being stuck in stone form for presumably many years, they are ready to go to battle against Perseus's enemies without even doing a bit of stretching.

This film has been somewhat forgotten, but this Medusa is one of the most underrated and creative monsters of cinema. Everything about her is perfect, from how she lurches forward, top first, propelled by the snakes at the base of her body, to the serpents whipping wildly around her eyes. She was an early work of special effects artist and creature creator Carlo Rambaldi, who would go on to win Academy Awards for his work, including for his design of *E.T. the Extra-Terrestrial* in 1982. His Medusa was a full-size animatronic, a towering, moving creature that was very advanced for special effects at the time, which would more commonly be done as a miniature or a man in a suit.

In 1964's *The Gorgon*, English film studio Hammer Films pulls the myth of Medusa out of ancient times and places her in the modern world, or rather, the world of 1910 Germany. The film begins with credits rolling over a gloomy shot of Castle Borski, then cuts to a painter creating a nude portrait of his gal. The two get into an argument, with her accusing him of not wanting to marry. After some back and forth, she reveals she is pregnant with his child. Oddly, he freaks out and runs away, saying he is going to talk to her father about the situation. She gives chase, but neither make it to their destination.

Later, she is brought to the village doctor, her body turned to stone, having been found in that state in the woods outside the castle. The painter is found not long after, hanging from a tree, bleeding from his face. He's thoroughly dead, but not turned to stone. The doctor and his assistant agree not to tell anyone about the woman's stone body and instead let the court posthumously declare she was murdered by the painter, who then hung himself.

The painter's father, believing his son is innocent, decides to investigate for himself. He speaks with the doctor, but the doctor doesn't say anything. However, the doctor is keeping a secret. This is not the first body found turned to stone. There are also whisperings that a Gorgon, here named Megaera instead of Medusa, has taken up residence in the castle.

The father decides to pay a visit to the castle. Director Terence Fisher, known for making lurid, brightly-colored monster movies for Hammer Films, here tones down the color. The palette is somber, with the interior of the castle being particularly gray and enshadowed. There are no warm orange fires burning like in the lair in *Clash of the Titans*, only strained, cold moonlight on the crumbling interior, the floor covered with dead leaves. The only splash of color is the green of the few plants that have made their way in and grow in some corners.

When Megaera appears from behind a mess of cobwebs, her emerald gown seems to glow in the darkness. While most monsters are happy to remain cloaked in shadows, she is incandescent, a beat of brightness amidst the castle's gloom. She shows herself for only a moment, barely long enough to glimpse her head of snakes, but long enough to turn the father into stone.

Soon, we learn more about Megaera from the doctor, who discusses the situation with his assistant, a young woman named Carla. He considers Megaera a creature of pure evil. Describing the ornaments atop her head, he says, "Each snake was a tentacle of the hellish brain from which it sprang." In all fairness though, she's only gorgonized trespassers in and around her castle. The doctor seems to know more than he is saying, and Carla can't understand why he won't talk about it.

Meanwhile, the painter's brother, Paul, shows up, presumably thinking that two members of his family have already been turned to stone so might as well go for three. He takes up the investigation, going to the little millhouse/artist studio where the painter and his girlfriend were last seen. While inside, the doors blow open. A gust of wind blows leaves inside. He goes out and rain begins to pour. He sees the reflection of Megaera in a pond. Again, she is ethereal. Her body seems to waiver in the downpour, dreamlike and wordless. She has saved him the trouble of coming to her castle, but this is a mere warning. He manages to avoid seeing her directly.

This isn't entirely a blessing. Paul wakes up in the hospital, where it is evident he is turning to stone, just more slowly than his brother and father. His hair is already gray. This is not enough to scare him off his investigation though. He calls in reinforcements, a professor friend. Together, they learn the murders began five years prior. That was the same time Carla moved to the village. Coincidence?

Of course it isn't. It turns out the spirit of Megaera has possessed Carla. On the full moon, the Gorgon possesses her body, apparently to hang out in the castle and wait for trespassers she can turn to stone. Carla never remembers these events, but the doctor has suspected the truth for some time, which is why he hasn't told anyone about the stone bodies. He wants to protect Carla.

The film reaches a climax with Paul and the doctor going to the castle, fighting with each other. So involved in their battle, they do not notice Megaera watching over them. She glows green, her snakes perched atop her head, hissing. Paul beats the doctor and finally becomes aware of Megaera. He keeps his eyes averted, watching in a large mirror as the Gorgon gracefully descends a flight of stairs to approach him. She stares at him with bloodshot eyes that peer from her scaled face.

When the Gorgon is focused on Paul, the professor shows up, sneaks behind Megaera and beheads her. Her head rolls to the floor. Her snakes recede. The scales peel from her face, revealing Carla's visage. This is the last thing Paul sees before he finally completes his transformation to stone.

The Gorgon is a moody, interesting take on Medusa's myth. The special effects are cheap and unambitious though, and hinder the finished product. Megaera's snakes are bobbling, rubbery and lifeless. In fact, the effects were so bad they inspired Ray Harryhausen to make sure his Medusa looked better. In an interview about *Clash of the Titans*, he says, "I always wanted to animate a Medusa, because I saw the Hammer film . . . and it was just a woman with rubber snakes in her hair, and every time she walked they would bounce! And I thought, oh God, you can't call that Medusa!"

Worse than the effects is how little justice the film does to the woman who portrays Megaera, Prudence Hyman. Hyman wasn't an actress, but a classically trained ballet dancer. She toured the UK and England with a number of travelling ballet companies, and also appeared in several musicals.

While she had appeared onscreen a few times previously in bit parts, *The Gorgon* was her first starring role. Unfortunately, she is not allowed to do anything beyond stand still for most of it, with only her descent down the stairs during the climax to hint at a lifetime of training her body to move. I imagine what could have been had Terence Fisher been more imaginative in his vision of her character, and freed her to swirl and move across the screen instead of serving as a pedestal for a poorly-designed snake effect.

Despite its shortcomings, *The Gorgon* does bring the myth of the Medusa into the modern world, hinting she has the power to become a monster suited for more than ancient times. But any woman with a Medusa tattoo could tell you how timeless the character truly is.

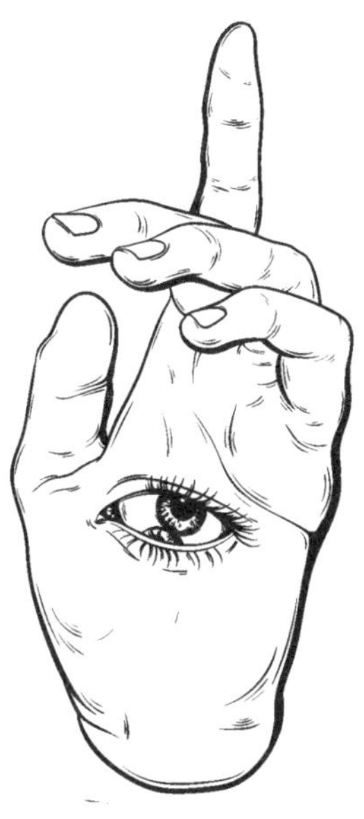

THE MAIDENS OF MIDIAN

In the night, a glimpse of a body hurtling through tall grass—a woman, naked, except for a coat of sharp quills on her back. She runs like an animal, on all fours. Others follow her, similarly inhuman. Screaming, gasping, and growling, they charge through swirling fog toward the gate of a cemetery.

As they get closer to the gate, what looked like panic now becomes a celebratory dance. The quilled woman writhes on the ground sensually. With a wicked smile, she reaches out a hand, beckoning all to join her as she makes her way through the gate. This is Shuna Sassi, of the Tribes of the Moon, the Nightbreed, and she has arrived at her home, Midian.

After this opening sequence, 1990's *Nightbreed* cuts to Aaron Boone, waking from sleep, believing what we have seen was a dream. It's one of many dreams of Midian that have come to him, so clearly he knows its history, how it's a place of refuge for monsters to hide from the humans who have persecuted them. He explains this to his lover, Lori, who comforts him.

While Boone dreams of monsters, a serial killer stalks suburbia. A man in a twisted mask with buttons for eyes and a zipper mouth is viciously slaughtering families. Fifteen people have been killed so far. When Boone next meets with Decker, his therapist, Decker tells Boone about these killings. He tells Boone that the people, places, and murders match what Boone has described in his dreams of Midian. He says Boone is the killer. He gives Boone some pills and tells him to report to the police.

Boone ends up in the hospital instead, after being nearly killed in a traffic accident. It turns out those pills were a powerful hallucinogen. At the hospital, Boone meets a raving man named Narcisse, who claims to know the location of Midian. He gives Boone directions before tearing off his own scalp, believing that is necessary to be accepted by the monsters of Midian.

In the frenzy created at the hospital by Narcisse's flesh-ripping, Boone escapes, heading toward Midian. Decker and the police are not far behind, however. Boone makes it to Midian. As he moves through the cemetery, he is discovered by Peloquin, a muscular Nightbreed with dreadlock-like tendrils hanging from his head, which he whips around as he transforms into his more animalistic, monstrous form. He hunts down and bites Boone.

Boone escapes and runs from the cemetery, only to be met by Decker and the police. Decker shouts that Boone has a gun and the police open fire. This time, Boone is killed. He's brought back to the morgue, where the medical examiner pulls bullet after bullet out of him. Thanks to Peloquin's bite though, Boone isn't dead in the typical sense. He is a monster now, a Nightbreed. He escapes the morgue and makes his way to Midian again.

There, the Tribes of the Moon accept him as one of their own. They bring him below ground, into the caverns beneath the cemetery, where the monsters live. They baptize him in the blood of Baphomet. When he enters the baptismal chamber for the ceremony, he is greeted by a group of Nightbreed, including Shuna Sassi. "I dreamt him," she shares, telling that Boone's dream at the outset of the film was no mere dream, but a true connection to her, and to Midian.

Shuna Sassi is a unique character in terms of her creation. Played by Christine McCorkindale, she was not in director and writer Clive Barker's book *Cabal,* upon which the movie is based, nor even in the screenplay. In the commentary for the director's cut, Barker reveals that early in production, the studio gave him the go-ahead to create four new monsters. He describes sitting down with conceptual artist Ralph McQuarrie for a sketch session to come up with the characters.

My greatest ever celebrity encounter was meeting Barker at Texas Frightmare Weekend, a horror convention. He did a sketch for me and I got to watch as he did it. Frenetically, he scribbled what at first seemed like random lines, but quickly came together into a character—a cigarette-smoking man with a small, second face on the side of his head.

While I watched Barker's drawing hand move wildly across paper, he spoke to me, explaining this character's background. He was so hurried to voice this story as it came to him I could hardly keep up. "This is a rogue character," he said. "Perhaps a Nightbreed, but more of a loner." The creative energy spilling out of Barker felt electric, wrapping me up. I battled between staying present in that moment to watch what was happening and drifting away to follow the character's journey in my mind, eventually settling somewhere in between.

So I can imagine what happened when Barker and McQuarrie went head-to-head in a brainstorming session. Like Barker, McQuarrie was a creative powerhouse, best known for the conceptual and promotional art he created for *Star Wars*, which was instrumental in getting the film produced. Together, they created Shuna Sassi.

A couple pieces of concept art exist as evidence of this session. First, a black and white sketch by Barker, clearly drawn at the same fevered pitch he drew in front of me at that convention, but a perfect representation of the character, quills and all. Second, a more fleshed-out, color illustration by McQuarrie, showing Boone and four Nightbreed, presumably the proposed new characters. They are clearly in early incarnations. Two are not easily matched with their final onscreen counterparts. One, Leroy Gomm, a strange character with two tendrils that emerge from his belly, is identifiable, but dramatically different from his onscreen incarnation. Shuna Sassi, however, is very similar to how she appears in the film.

Despite only having one line, McCorkindale makes Shuna Sassi one of the most memorable characters in the film, and my favorite, perhaps my favorite monster of all time. She came to the film with no previous movie experience. A dancer, she was training in physical theater with David Glass. Glass was in charge of creature choreography for the film, and a bit of a legend in the world of theater.

Through movement, with only seconds on screen, McCorkindale tells a story of a character who loves her body, who understands its power, not only in terms of sensuality, but in terms of the deadliness of her quills. She moves confidently and rhythmically, as if life itself is a dance. Even in moments of stillness, she seems to flow with everything around her, in contrast to some of the other members of the Tribes of the Moon, who push against the edges of reality, rather than move with it.

While some sequences, such as the opening dream dance, are not given much screentime, in *Tribes of the Moon: The Making of Nightbreed*, the documentary about the making of the film, we can see the choreography being practiced, both in and out of costume, and it's clear how much time was spent to create that sequence, which sets the stage for the Nightbreed's physicality and movement and relation to their surroundings.

As Boone is below ground being baptized into the Tribes of the Moon, Lori is above ground searching for him. As she moves through the maze of monuments and overgrowth, she encounters an animal lying on its side, unable to move, struggling for breath. This is unlike any other animal Lori has seen, and she is hesitant to approach. From inside a nearby tomb, a woman calls out, asking Lori to bring the animal to her. Lori does, lifting this struggling animal and carrying her to the shadows of the tomb. In the mysterious woman's arms, the animal transforms, becomes human.

The child is Babette, and the woman is her mother, Rachel. Rachel, portrayed by Catherine Chevalier, is a unique member of the Nightbreed in that she is human in appearance. In her floral lace cloak, with long black hair wrapped in metallic sheaths, she's what "naturals" (the term the Nightbreed use for boring human people) would refer to as beautiful. In fact, her conventional beauty is subject to a bit of discrimination among the rest of the Nightbreed. According to *The Nightbreed Chronicles*, the film's companion book, they consider her looks pitiful. "Behind her back they call her 'The Hostage,' though whether this is to love or symmetry, no one will say."

Told she cannot go below to see Boone, Lori is

frightened away by some of the other, less symmetrical, Nightbreed. But when she steps outside of the gates, thinking she's made it to safety, she encounters the serial killer, Buttonface, and his blades. He reveals that he is Decker, Boone's therapist, and chases her back into Midian. There, Boone arises to save her. He succeeds, only to have the police arrive, who manage to capture him and bring him to jail, where the smalltown doctor panics upon discovering Boone does not have a pulse.

Rachel and Lori, along with Narcisse, who is now a member of the Nightbreed, stage a jailbreak. This is where Rachel proves her membership in the Tribes of the Moon. Transforming into a cloud of smoke, she seeps through the lockup door.

Once inside, she reconfigures into her human form. Naked, she stands in front of the guard. He is stunned. Whether it is by her transformation or her beauty, it matters not.

"I do not want to hurt you," she lies sweetly, before pressing her lips to his, reaching into him in smoke form and snuffing out his life. He falls away, dead.

"Naughty, naughty," Narcisse chides the guard's corpse, smoke still pouring from his mouth.

They free Boone and hurry back to Midian in their rusty old hearse. Unfortunately, the police are already en route, set on destroying Midian and everything hiding there, and they've enlisted a firepower-loving, redneck militia called the Sons of Freedom to help. Their act of terrorism begins as soon as they reach the cemetery. They set fires. They blow things up. They kill Nightbreed like it's a game. In the midst of this, Decker wreaks destruction with his blades. Some Nightbreed hide. Others flee. A few fight.

When one trigger-happy redneck points a gun at Babette as Lori cradles her in her arms, Rachel sneaks up behind him. Turning her arm to smoke, she reaches through his chest. She reforms her arm to solid flesh and then yanks it from his body, an elegant method of execution.

Elsewhere, a group of militia men are standing around the flaming ruins, laughing over the body of a Nightbreed they have murdered. One is struck in the neck by a short quill. Screaming, he pulls it out.

"I don't feel so good," he says, before falling to the ground.

One of the remaining men goes to his knees to look after his fallen comrade. The other turns to see where the quill came from. Shuna Sassi emerges from the shadows of a tomb, opening her crimson robe to reveal her bare breasts. She pants lustily and the man follows her as she slips back into her hiding place. Catching her, he peels her robe from her shoulder, revealing her back thick with long quills. She launches them at him, and they dig deep into his face as he cries out. She runs out and dispatches the remaining man as easily, whipping her quills in a little dance while laughing over his dying body.

Despite her animal-like body, Shuna Sassi exudes sexuality, which she learned to weaponize against humans long ago. According to *The Nightbreed Chronicles*, she spent the 1930s working in Boston's most notorious brothel. The clients who chose her knew they were courting death. "One misguided caress would undoubtedly result in a terrible demise." On a whim, she killed at least one man who visited her, or so she says. When monsters tell their origins, it is to be taken with a grain of salt. In his introduction, Barker explains that many of the breed will offer any number of origin stories if asked. As many lifetimes as some of them have lived, they can be forgiven for forgetting the details, or amusing themselves with a fresh origin once the previous has gone stale.

As the battle between humans and monsters rages on, Boone and Decker have their final confrontation. Boone emerges the victor, gathering the surviving Nightbreed to flee and take refuge in a nearby barn, eventually to begin the search for a new home.

Clive Barker was the first author whose work I fell in love with, though I was only a preteen when I started reading his books. When I rented *Nightbreed* from the video store, I fell in love with that too. If there's ever been a monster movie more epic in scope, with such extensive history and lore, and as many monsters, I have yet to see it. It's a monster fangirl's dream.

As I got older, I learned Barker was not happy with the movie I saw, the theatrical cut, which I have described here. It had been butchered by the studio, who didn't understand the concept of monsters being the good guys. Barker explains the studio's mindset: "You don't talk about monsters as interesting, or emotionally, creatively, or theologically rich creatures. Sympathetic. You just beat them up or burn them."

More than two decades after the film's release, Barker fans started digging for the original cut. They were given the runaround by studio executives. Eventually though, the missing footage was found. Initially, it was pieced together by fans into *The Cabal Cut*, which includes basically everything recorded, including a love scene between Shuna Sassi and Peloquin on a bed full of snakes. Then, the footage was used to create Clive Barker's director's cut, much more aligned with the novel and the script, not to mention the filmmaker's intent. It's a beautiful thing. There's more monster footage. Voices the studio strangely overdubbed were restored.

Perhaps it's nostalgia, but I don't view these newly-found visions as replacements for the theatrical cut, but additions. I'm not about to discard the version of the film I fell in love with, flaws and all. Every version is worth watching. Maybe it was me being someone who wanted to empathize with monsters, having often been treated like one, but despite the studio-butchering, I saw the intent. I saw the monsters as the heroes, and I loved them for it.

Some viewers see the monsters as more than heroes. *Nightbreed* is often interpreted as a queer metaphor, with the Nightbreed as the queer folks and humans as the straight society that persecutes them and forces them into the shadows. There's compelling reason for this interpretation, not the least of which is that the book and film were created by a gay man at the height of the AIDS epidemic. Boone coming to Midian and becoming a Nightbreed could be read as him coming to terms with his queerness. The Nightbreed themselves are a chosen family, so much like those that LGBTQ+ people find and grow for lack of support from their birth families. Then, of course, is the whole living in the shadows element.

It's a lovely and valid interpretation. For me, I see a broader representation of societal outcasts, and Barker has described it as such. After all, he never shied away from writing queer stories overtly. *Sacrament*, for example, deals with a character navigating his queerness while watching his friends die from the plague. Everything Barker writes is inherently queer, making it hard for me to believe he'd couch a tale of queer life in metaphor. Then again, it's up to the viewers to create the meaning.

I used to say that I love horror movies. Not anymore. Now I tell people I love monster movies, and *Nightbreed* is the best illustration of that distinction. Its primary purpose is not to horrify, but to tell a story about beings with different bodies. Sometimes monsters are scary, for sure. More often, they are not. They have lives and hearts that, despite their physical selves, are often as complex and hurt as any human's. Many times they are victims—abused, manipulated, used. While their violent acts may not always be justified, monsters are surprisingly human.

CONCLUSION: EQUAL RIGHTS, EQUAL BITES

Monster movies have historically come in waves, starting in the 30s with the Universal Studios monsters like Dracula, Frankenstein, and the Bride. Then monsters disappeared for a decade or so before climbing to prominence again in the 50s. Most recently, the 80s saw another boom, delivering some of the weirdest and grossest monsters in the history of horror.

In recent decades, monster movies have struggled against more realistic horrors like slashers and cannibals, not to mention the budgets required for good special effects. With war seemingly everywhere and propaganda telling us immigrants will take our jobs and queer people will harm our families, it's no surprise home invasion movies have become such a huge subgenre in the horror field. Why worry about Draculas coming to suck our blood when everywhere around us, forces are supposedly working to uproot us from our homes and our lifestyles?

But perhaps it is exactly Draculas who we need to fear. In his cultural history of horror films, *The Monster Show*, David J. Skal argues Dracula was the perfect monster for the depression era. The bloodsucking aristocrat functioned as a stand-in for the capitalists that drained bank accounts, getting rich while everyone else suffered. Dracula is due for a comeback.

And who's to say Dracula can't be a woman? We need another monster movie wave, and with more women taking up creative space writing and directing horror films, the time is ripe for a takeover of ghoulish femmes. We are all sick of women being the primary victims, and being the hero is fun and all, but is representation meaningful if we aren't represented in all roles? Even the gross, ooze-y ones?

As this book has demonstrated, there's a legacy of monstrous women, from Medusa to the Bride to the She-Creature to the Wasp Woman. They've blazed a trail with tooth and claw, showing that they can be everything that their monstrous male counterparts can be and more, often telling stories and expressing meanings that are distinctly femme.

It's time to take back the term "scream queen," flip it, and redefine it. Let's stop being the queens who do the screaming, and start being the ones who cause those screams!

SOURCES AND FURTHER READING

Introduction

"Famous Monsters of Filmland." *Grand Comic Database.* https://www.comics.org/series/1425/covers/?page=1.

Sontag, S. (1966). "Against Interpretation." *Against Interpretation.* Farrar, Straus, and Giroux.

The Original Woman

Palmer, R. (1997). *Paul Blaisdell, Monster Maker.* McFarland.

The Many Brides of Frankenstein

Harmon, J. & Bresee, F. (1975). "The Golden Days of Frankenstein." *Monsters of the Movies.* https://monstermemories.blogspot.com/2008/09/bride-interview-article.html.

Poovey, M. (1984). "My Hideous Progeny: The Lady and the Monster." *The Proper Lady and the Woman Writer: Ideology as Style in the Works of Mary Wollstonecraft, Mary Shelley, and Jane Austen.* University of Chicago Press.

The Art History Lesson (with Fangs)

Pelley, R. (2022, September 17). "Grace Jones: 'Even if I stand on my head, I still can't do it. How these young girls twerk, I don't know.' " *The Guardian.* https://www.theguardian.com/lifeandstyle/2022/sep/17/this-much-i-know-grace-jones-how-these-young-girls-twerk-i-dont-know.

Stace, C.L. (n.d.). "Artistic Collaborations: Keith Haring & Grace Jones." *Artland Magazine.*

https://magazine.artland.com/keith-haring-grace-jones-collaboration/

The Today Show. (1986, July). https://www.youtube.

com/watch?v=eKzjpKCbmLo.

The Werewolf Sisters

Evans, W. (1973). "Monster Movies: A Sexual Theory." *The Journal of Popular Film.* https://www.researchgate.net/publication/303289839_Monster_Movies_A_Sexual_Theory_The_Journal_of_Popular_Film_II_Fall_1973_353-365.

Henery, M. (2020). "Interview: Karen Walton's 'Ginger Snaps' Offers a Horror Renewal." *Fangoria.* https://certifiedforgotten.com/ginger-snaps-uterus-horror.

Red Carpet News. (2019, February 20). "Katharine Isabelle Shares Her True Feelings About Horror." https://www.youtube.com/watch?v=VCr7EhqGmlU.

The Living Dead Girl

Lauro, S.J. & Embry, K. (2008). "A Zombie Manifesto:The Nonhuman Condition in the Era of Advanced Capitalism." *Boundary.* https://www.thing.net/~rdom/ucsd/Zombies/ZombieManifesto.pdf.

The Girl in the Well

Quint. (2005, January 26). "Quint interviews original RINGU and current RING TWO director Hideo Nakata!!!" *Ain't It Cool News.* http://legacy.aintitcool.com/node/19252.

Suzuki, K. (1991). *Ring*. Kadokawa Shoten.

Totaro, D. (2000, July). "The 'Ring' Master: Interview with Hideo Nakata." *Off Screen*. https://offscreen.com/view/hideo_nakata.

The Nazi Killer

Brehmer, N. (2021). *Puppet Master Complete: A Franchise History*. McFarland.

Zimmer, C. (2006, February 7). "His Subject: Highly Evolved and Exquisitely Thirsty." *The New York Times*.

https://www.nytimes.com/2006/02/07/science/his-subject-highly-evolved-and-exquisitely-thirsty.html.

The Beasts of Beauty

Budrewicz, M. (2020, August 26). "The Convoluted Tale of Evil Spawn." *Schlock Pit*. https://theschlockpit.com/2020/08/26/convoluted-tale-evil-spawn-1987/.

The Genetics Society. (2021, June 3). "A Growth Industry: The Story of Human Growth Hormone." *Genetics Unzipped*. https://geneticsunzipped.com/transcripts/2021/6/3/a-growth-industry-the-story-of-human-growth-hormone.

Grow, B., & Shiffman, J. (2017, October 24). "In the U.S. Market for Human Bodies, Almost Anyone Can Dissect and Sell the Dead." *Reuters*. https://

www.reuters.com/investigates/special-report/usa-bodies-brokers/.

Han, S.M., & et al. (2015, October 1). "The Beneficial Effects of Honeybee-Venom Serum on Facial Wrinkles in Humans. *National Library of Medicine.* https://pmc.ncbi.nlm.nih.gov/articles/PMC4598227/.

"Human Growth Hormone (HGH): Does It Slow Aging?" *Mayo Clinic.* https://www.mayoclinic.org/healthy-lifestyle/healthy-aging/in-depth/growth-hormone/art-20045735

Klunder, J. (1987, June 7). "Bizarre Lives Bared of Star, Son Accused of Her Murder." *Los Angeles Times.* https://www.latimes.com/archives/la-xpm-1987-06-07-me-923-story.html.

Moore, J. (2018, January 12). "CIA Files Reveal Jordan's King Hussein May Have Had Child With Jewish Hollywood Actress." *Newsweek.* https://www.newsweek.com/cia-files-reveal-jordans-king-hussein-had-child-jewish-hollywood-actress-779375.

Mysteries & Scandals. (2000, August 7). Episode 155: Susan Cabot.

Ramati-Ziber, L. Shnabel, N., & Glick, P. (2019, August). "The Beauty Myth: Prescriptive Beauty Norms for Women Reflect Hierarchy-Enhancing Motivations Leading to Discriminatory Employment Practices." *Journal of Personality &*

Social Psychology. https://gap.hks.harvard.edu/beauty-myth-prescriptive-beauty-norms-women-reflect-hierarchyenhancing-motivations-leading.

Suh, E. (2024, September 18). " 'The Movie Is Fundamentally About the Violence of Control': Writer-Director Coralie Fargeat Talks *The Substance.*" *Vogue.* https://www.vogue.com/article/coralie-fargeat-the-substance-interview/.

The Snake-Haired Woman

Culpepper, E. (1986). "Ancient Gorgons: A Face for Contemporary Women's Rage." *Woman of Power Magazine.*

Tasker, A. (2022, February 23). "Ray Harryhausen Talks About His Cinematic Magic." *American Cinematographer.* https://theasc.com/articles/ray-harryhausen-talks-about-his-cinematic-magic/.

The Maidens of Midian

Barker, C. (1988). *Cabal.* Poseidon Press

Barker, C. (1989). *The Nightbreed Chronicles.* Titan Books.

Danhauser, R. (2014, November 29). Episode 86: Chris McCorkindale with Michael Plumides. *Clive Barker Podcast.* https://clivebarkercast.com/2014/11/29/episode-86-chris-mccorkindale-with-michael-plumides/.

Conclusion

Skal, David J. (1993). *The Monster Show: A Cultural History of Horror*. W. W. Norton & Co.

ABOUT THE AUTHOR

Emma Alice Johnson grows wildflowers and writes. She lives on a farm dedicated to conservation of native plants and endangered insects. She has released a number of zines, chapbooks, and micro press and art press novellas. Her short fiction has appeared in more than 75 publications, including *Dark Matter Presents Human Monsters, The Dark, Dark Discoveries,* and other dark places. When she isn't planting or writing, she can be found running through the woods with her pet pig, singing to her chickens, lifting weights, watching B-movies, or reading while snuggled with her cat. Learn more at http://www.freaktension.com.